ARE YOU READY TO DO SO?

TADIMALLA H MOHAN RAO

ISBN 979-8-88959-695-0

I Dedicate
This Maiden & Modest Effort
Of Mine
To
My Late Mother
Sundaramma
Who Was
An Epitome of Patience,
Serenity,
&
Eternal Values

Contents

Preface

"Are You Ready To Do So?" ..., I am always enthralled by this beautiful phrase. And I always wanted to pose this question to people whenever any effort I undertook was instrumental in positively addressing their genuine concerns and thus caused true jubilation in them. Over a period, without my active knowledge, I was actually putting this thought into practice and most of those the question had been posed to, are in fact responding with a gleeful *yes*!

Above continuous affirmations from people far and near had encouraged me to crystallize my resultant reflections into words and I slowly started attempting to write on the issues concerning the day-to-day life and especially, those revolving around human ethics and values, embracing, or discarding of which, the human life either makes or breaks. Gradually my interest took a turn towards understanding the tangibles as well as intangibles (more so, the intangibles) that elevate human life and alleviate human strife.

As my interest was getting deeper, I picked up the strength to look beyond the horizon of the diverse human psyche I was exposed to, and through the robust Public Sector corporate structure, I was in. I tried to give a proper and relevant shape to my modest thoughts by truthfully trying to understand various concerns of people around me and attempted to arrive at possible solutions that could probably address their concerns and put them at ease. This honest effort went on seriously for three years from 2018 to 2021 (though sporadically prevalent earlier too), starting from one year prior to my retirement (in July 2019) to two years post my retirement from the corporate office of the Nagpur-based Western Coalfields Ltd (WCL), a subsidiary of Coal India Ltd (CIL), the Maharatna Central Public Sector Enterprise functioning under the administrative control of the Ministry of Coal, Govt of India.

The gratifying outcome of the 3-year effort is this little book, a cohesive pack of 12 articles and 2 real-life stories, under the genre non-fiction. While the articles encompass a deeper penetration into the subject of human ethics & values, the real-life stories are the true stories that depict the consumer and woman power at their best. Besides, while one article *Managers Vs Damagers,* attempts to focus on the prerequisites required for managerial/leadership positioning, another aims to address the concerns associated with modern maladies. And yet other endeavors to shed light on the Nagpur-based Hislop College, one of the 18 colleges in India on which the University Grants Commission conferred the rare 'Special Heritage Status' in 2015, on completion of 125 years of its glorious existence.

I am delighted to make a particular mention about three exquisite books, amongst others, that greatly helped me in acquiring a deep insight into the nuances of understanding the human and scientific temper in relation to my modest effort. These literary jewels are:

1. ***The Impact of Science on Society*** *authored by Nobel Laureate Earl Bertrand Russell, and published by Unwin Books/London in 1952*

2. ***Human Values in Management*** *authored by Swami Ranganathananda, globally renowned and widely respected scholar-monk of the Ramakrishna Order, thinker, and eloquent speaker on the spiritual and cultural aspects of life, and published by Coal India Ltd/Kolkata in 1986, and*

3. ***Ignited Minds-Unleashing the Power within India*** *authored by Dr APJ Abdul Kalam, our nation's much respected 11*[th] *President (2002-2007), and fondly remembered as the People's President, our own missile man, a scientist par excellence, and a seer, who had*

perfectly justified our nation's foray into the nuclear world by saying strength respects strength (when he encountered a question from an inquisitive journalist as to how this peace-loving country has gone nuclear), and published by Penguin Books/New Delhi in 2002.

During the 5-decade long period from 1952 to 2002, the above three books adored the world literary firmament at three different & distinct times and stamped their well-defined authority on the global literary world ever since. It is amazing that the books, despite the huge gap between the years of their publication (3 ½ decades between the first and second, and 1 ½ decades between the second and third), and having dealt with altogether different subjects, had one thing in common, emphasis on *human orientation!* It's my privilege to state that I have enormously and repeatedly drawn from the in-built flavour and fragrance of the above three literary jewels that had immensely enriched the intent and content of the articles. Further, one article in particular, *Wellness in Illness*, contains a conscious sprinkle of a liberal quantity of alliterations, as demanded by its contours. Though a small experiment from the hilarious angle, the content did fit into the context well. I believe, the effort would find favour with the critic in the reader.

Initial versions of two articles *Life Without Life* and *Crime and Corruption* earlier appeared in WCL's in-house publications *Parivartan* and *Pahal* brought out by the company's Vigilance Department on the occasion of the Vigilance Awareness Week Celebrations held during 2014 and 2015 respectively. Further, the initial version of another article *Ethical Leadership* also found its place earlier in another in-house publication of the Nagpur Chapter of the Indian Institute of Materials Management brought out on the occasion of the 2-day Seminar on *Ethical Leadership from Vigilance Perspective for sustainable excellence*, conducted at Hotel Centre Point/Nagpur from 21 to 22 April 2018. Thus, the period of the last (close to) 7 ½ years (from April 2012 to July 2019) of my career at WCL Hq/Nagpur was more etched in my memory as the period of my modest pursuit with the pen and is fondly remembered as my maiden *literary* phase!

The preface would not be complete if a revered mention was not made to *Shri K.P. Jaisal* and the *Sheroes*, who had figured in this book. Jaisal is a 32-year-old fisherman from Tanur, Kerala, who had practically become a human bridge in the service of flood-hit people. Kneeling on all his four (hands and knees) in the murky waters during the August 2018 floods that ravaged the State, Jaisal physically made his back a steppingstone to help women and children (with their footwear on) climb over him onto the waiting rescue boat for safety.

The *sheroes* (she heroes) are the brave woman warriors who, with matchless grit and determination, effectively fought the brutal acid attacks perpetuated against them by rogue elements from family and society. Bouncing back on their feet to pursue life with dignity, the *stars with the scars* are into successfully running a restaurant in Agra, aptly named *Sheroes Hangout*, a true reflection of the invincible woman power. While Jaisal had figured in the article *Barriers Vs Bridges*, the real-life story *Sheroes of Agra* is all about the sheroes.

I am highly indebted to Shri K. Padmanabhaiah, IAS (Rtd), former Home Secretary, Govt of India, and currently, Chairman, Court of Governors/ASCI (Administrative Staff College of India), Hyderabad, for his kind congratulatory message sent to me in response to my email addressed to him informing about my proposed plans for publication of my articles & real-life stories in a book form. Hand-picked by PV as the Home Secretary, he soon became the messiah of J&K Affairs and played a crucial role in reviving the political process in the trouble-torn state by paving the way for holding the Legislative Assembly elections in 1996 after a gap of 9 years in the insurgency-ridden state. He is the recipient of the Shiromani and Priyadarshini Awards in 1996 for National Development & Integration, and Outstanding Public Service respectively. In 2008, he was bestowed with the Padma Bhushan. After retirement in 1997 he was appointed as the ***Government of India***

Representative for holding the Naga peace talks, which led to a ceasefire and a complete return of peace in Nagaland. His congratulatory message provided me with the necessary energy to take my work forward, to the Publisher's desk.

A few phrases mentioned in some of the articles were sourced from the exquisite audio tapes containing profound teachings of seasoned leaders belonging to the Britt Worldwide Education System. I express my sincere gratitude to all those amazing Britt leaders for, every word that flew from their mouths was a pearl of wisdom! I could have access to those remarkable tapes as my wife was a student of the Britt School during the tenure of my posting at the Regional Sales Office/CIL/ Chennai. Any Britt student, who would read this book, can easily figure out those phrases. And those who are not, can also equally easily figure out the phrases from the in-depth meaning and value they contain!

All the articles & real-life stories end with the phrase *Are You Ready To Do So?,* which is a direct question to the readers. This is an attempt to check whether the readers are ready to do as suggested in each of the articles & real-life stories in the event they encounter the different issues/situations summarized therein, in their real lives. I am extremely happy to keep the same phrase as the *title* of this book.

I am sure, a journey through this book from cover to cover would provide the readers with an everlasting experience that is both engrossing and eyebrow-raising. Critical comments and candid feedback from the readers add enormous value to my literary wealth and hence are a great welcome.

– Tadimalla Hanuma Mohan Rao
Hyderabad
Date: Feb 04, 2023
e-mail: mohan.th2260@gmail.com
Mobile/WhatsApp: 94055 88823

Acknowledgments

My life-long indebtedness, primarily, to my late mother Sundaramma, an epitome of patience, serenity, and eternal values, for raising me with undying ideals and principles right from my early age, and who left this world in her late eighties.

To my wife, Surya Kumari, a classical vocalist & Veena instrumentalist, for her sagacious advice to me to give a vivid shape in writing to my life's experience and for her firm support throughout, now over 3 decades.

To my brother-in-law, Shri Pandrangi Ananda Surya Prasad, former HoD, Legal Department/SECL (South Eastern Coalfields Ltd, another subsidiary of CIL), my career-mentor, a voracious reader & prized writer, and a cherished pen friend of Nobel Laureate Earl Bertrand Russell (1872-1970), Playwright and Novelist Somerset Maugham (1874-1965), the Right Honorable Lord Denning* (1899-1999), and

---

* Lord Denning, hailed as the greatest English judge of modern times happened to be in Nagpur in the company of the former Chief Justice of India, Justice Hidayatullah, during His Lordship's visit to India in Jan 1976 to deliver VV Chitaley Memorial Law Lectures at the invitation of the Trustees of The VV Chitaley Memorial Law Lectureship Endowment Committee. Under the Lecture Series, Lord Denning delivered three lectures – one at Bombay on 1st Jan 1976 on the subject "Changing the Law", the second at Nagpur on 3rd Jan 1976 on the subject "The New Equity", and the third at Delhi on 5th Jan 1976 on the subject "Let Justice be Done" (Source: All India Reporter Pvt Ltd/Nagpur's article published in Cr LJ 1976).

Shri Prasad had the rare privilege of personally meeting Lord Denning during the latter's Nagpur visit. During the subsequent personal interaction that ensued, to Shri Prasad's query as to how he could write such utterly

Swami Pranavananda* (1896-1989), FRGS, amongst other literary and legal luminaries from India and abroad, for propping me up in life, introducing me to his vast & priceless library, for sharing with me the close to 3-decade long personal correspondence the first three British legends had with him, including their autographed photographs, and for planting the early seeds in me to relish the enormous beauty of the world of books that greatly helped me to develop a passion for writing.

---

simple English, Lord Denning replied with a little laugh that it was the most challenging task! Later, in one of his letters to Shri Prasad, Lord Denning was fondly remembering his Nagpur visit and his interaction with Shri Prasad. While writing the most difficult tracts of law, Lord Denning's English never went beyond high school standard. He believed that law was meant for ordinary people and not scholars. He came to be known as the world's greatest judge of the 20th Century. He was even promptly responding to postcards sent to him by people in their case matters and did not care for form but right administration of justice (Source: Shri Prasad's memoirs).

*   Swami Pranavananda (earlier name Kanakadandi Venkata Somayajulu) hailed from the East Godavari District of the then-combined State of Andhra Pradesh. He was the unusual combination of an ascetic, a born explorer and a passionate geographer, all put into one. In the course of his total 23-year wanderings in the Himalayan hermitages during his journeys in Tibet, he made several trips to Mt. Kailash and Manasarovar, and on each occasion undertook a *parikrama* or circumambulation of the mountain and lake, precisely 23 circumambulations of Mt Kailash and 25 of Manasarovar, and fixed the sources of four major rivers - the Indus, the Karnali (a tributary of Ganges), the Brahmaputra and the Sutlej, in the process exploding the nearly 3-decade old findings of Dr Sven Hedin, the Swedish explorer, which evoked great sensation among the Himalayan Geographers all over the world. In recognition of his outstanding contribution to the geography of the region, Swami Pranavananda was conferred with the Fellowship of the Royal Geographical Society (Source: Swami Pranavananda's 1949 publication titled "History of Kailash and Manasarovar" with a foreword by Pt Jawaharlal Nehru).

To my sister, Smt. Pandrangi Hanumayamma, Sr. Accounts Officer-Rtd/WCL, for her value-studded guidance at every turn of my close to 37 ½ years of career in WCL/CIL.

To my eldest neice, Smt. Kesiraju Venkata Subba Lakshmi, for providing me a graceful picture of my mother.

To my two sons - Ravi Teja, twice-published author, a social commerce entrepreneur, and presently working as an editing lead in a Hyderabad-based Digital Media & Commerce Company (incNut Digital), engaged in digital content creation on topics pertaining to health, wellness, and beauty, and Sasi Kanth, a budding web developer working with another Hyderabad-based Digital Services Startup (Purple Syntax Digital), engaged in digital marketing, web & app development, and graphic designing services - for their unstinted support in first creating a perfect ambiance for me to write, and then in helping me to crystallize the ideas through absorbing discussions.

To all my other siblings, relatives, friends, former superiors & colleagues at the Hqrs of WCL & CIL, and Smt. G. Vijayalaxmi, my former senior colleague at the Regional Sales Office, CIL, Chennai and her husband, Shri J. Ganeshen, a Chartered Accountant, and a highly resourceful person ever-ready to extend support - for their enormous affection, eternal wisdom, and perpetual guidance that steered my life to a perfect shore.

To the TV-9 Telugu Channel for airing that stunning reality show on the Sheroes of Agra one night around 9.30 during Sept 2015 (if I rightly remember), without which I wouldn't have ever been able to meet the "Sheroes", the unbeatable stars with the scars.

Finally to Notion Press, Chennai, for offering splendid and wholesome services for publication.

ARTICLES

[On Human Ethics And Values]

1

Life Without Life

In all our daily lives, there is always an indispensable need to reflect *clarity, transparency, and honesty* in whatever we think, express, and act upon. These three vital values form the base on which the entire healthy human edifice stands, and a robust business prospers. Unfortunately, many a time, we notice a lot of *chaos and confusion* everywhere in the environment we are in. Though these two damaging elements continuously bar us from absorbing the above three finest human qualities and thus hinder us from practicing them, we seldom do anything to keep these two harmful elements at bay.

Because of our pathetic inaction, we are becoming directly or indirectly responsible for the vicious harm they bring along. Why don't we rise to the occasion and effectively respond to the above situation though we are fully aware of their detrimental consequences? The reasons, sadly and badly are:

a. we are already a part of the system that is devoid of the first-mentioned three vital life-making and life-changing values, and

b. we are brazenly habituated to allowing the next mentioned two disgusting elements to continue to happen around us

And the cycle of decay sets in and spirals its rapid spread. Here is how it goes...

As highly *experienced, educated,* and *intelligent* race as we always claim ourselves to be, knowingly or unknowingly, we often tend to start our day in *chaos and confusion*, discharge our functions through the day in *chaos and confusion* and also end our day in *chaos and confusion.*

The cost of our embracing these two destructive elements all through the day and beyond is forcing many of us to spend many a sleepless night, snatching away a night's happy sleep from us. The wretched state keeps on continuing 24 X 7 for many days, weeks, and sometimes even months and years....

Before you take notice of the damage that is being caused to you, it is already too late... Result? Depression arising out of insomnia, irritation, and consequent anger grips you, making you prone to many new-age health disorders, which take a severe toll on your mental as well as physical health. Effect? A typical situation follows the next day also, the day after that, and so on endlessly..., in the process, fully draining the energy out of you, making you non-productive, non-qualitative and dead-wood like, leaving you look like a live cadaver, taking the glitter away from your life, forcing you to lead a *LIFE WITHOUT LIFE*.

How to get out of this situation? How to bring the lost "life" back into your life and rebuild your life with life? The solution, though not difficult, is not simple either and with a focussed mind, definitely *NOT* impossible. Here is how the solution unfolds:

First and foremost, start your day with a lot of ecstasy. Enjoy the early morning breeze, the walk you embark on by the lakeside in the soothing company of the rising crimson Sun, and the breakfast you eat along with your family members. Try to bring in basics into your daily work. Stronger the basics, faster the perception. Understanding the basics helps you in getting rid of chaos and confusion. As chaos and confusion leave, *CLARITY* sets in, which is the first dimension on which the healthy human edifice stands, and a robust business prospers. Begin your daily work with clarity of thought, clarity of purpose, and clarity about the process that is to be followed. Then, *ETP*, i.e., *Enjoy The Process*. Whatever you do, enjoy the process. Whatever you think and act upon, be sure that you are delivering your best 100%. Try to find joy in anything and everything either you take up on your own or that is entrusted to you.

Second, continue your work with renewed ecstasy. Then, *RTB*, i.e., *Raise The Bar*. You are the one, who knows your 100%, i.e., *no one knows you better than you*. You know your true strengths. Yet, you are the one who imposes 100% limitations on you. *Break the shackles of self-made constraints.* Enhance your working skills by enhancing your learning skills and blow off the cap you yourself have set on your expertise. Raise your bar by unearthing your latent energy. Let your new-found energy flow through your mind and body. *Fortunately, you are your maximum and unfortunately, you are also your minimum.* Just erase the word 'minimum' from the frame of your mind. Keep your mind open to new ideas. As learned from history, three things function to their optimum, only when they are open. A Parachute, an Umbrella, and the Human Mind. Let your mind not remain shut when you transact your business.

Keep the window of your mind open so that the fresh and gentle breeze runs across carrying refreshingly new and vibrant thoughts. Consciously wipe out the word 'hush-hush' from your word list. Keep the shady deals away from the threshold of your doorstep. As this dreadful word leaves your domain, another stunning word, TRANSPARENCY, the second dimension on which the healthy human edifice stands, and a robust business prospers, takes birth, leading to openness in your transactions creating a spectacular global phenomenon out of you. Be transparent in whatever you think, express, and act upon. The world returns you back in the same coin and in full measure.

Third, with the help of the now new-found ecstasy, *WTT and TTW*, i.e., *Walk The Talk and Talk The Walk*. By stating so, I mean that you should only do what you say and only say what you do, like the Mahatma. These two actions of *doing and saying,* and *saying and doing* are concurrently not possible, unless *HONESTY*, the third dimension on which the healthy human edifice stands, and a robust business prospers, becomes the watchword in your life. As the old adage *honesty is the best policy* goes, practice this third great human quality to the hilt, till it becomes a habit. As you build honesty into your character, this great quality becomes your way of life. When honesty is intertwined with the other two great human qualities, viz., clarity and transparency, then these three great human assets together take the shape of a gigantic force. After that, this colossal energy transforms the appalling, insensitive, and fraudulent human residing inside you bent to carry out dubious deals, into an all-caring and finest individual.

This transformed human surfaced out of you will now be inclined to undertake only clear deals, ready to perform righteous functions without any *chaos or confusion*, and with a definite purpose and precision, aimed at the absolute betterment of the organization/ society you are in. The beacon that is lit inside you because of this great transformation also shows the way to millions, guiding them to their respective destinations through the numerous maze-like paths strewn with sharp spikes of *chaos and confusion*, putting their lost 'life' also back into their lives.

The dawn of such a great society can be a definite reality, which ushers in better days free from all social ills, transforming you from your earlier *life without life* situation to the well-deserved *life with life* situation, bringing the glitter back into your life, making your life radiant with life... therefore, in order to have this radiant life, it is essential that you incorporate the three finest human values, viz., clarity, transparency, and honesty into your system of functioning at each and every functional level.

It's time to take this important decision NOW, and simultaneously act upon it by putting your heart and soul into it! Are You Ready To Do So?

--//--

2

Wellness In Illness

The Crucial Questions: Why only *a few* people are endowed with a good number of strengths that empower them to fight the many ills that surround them? Why only *a few* people are capable of finding everything vivid and dazzling even in a gloomy situation? Why only *a few* people are able to spot an opportunity in every adversity? Why only *a few* people emerge as true leaders and reach the top rung of the success ladder? And, why only *a few* people always see wellness even in their worst illness? Now, let's try to take questions for the people at the other end of the scale. Why only *the majority* of people always succumb to pressures and fail to confront the odds? Why only *the majority* of people always become victims of their own-making and meekly surrender to the circumstances? Why only *the majority* of people always fail to spot an opportunity even in decidedly favourable circumstances? Why only *the majority of* people forever remain part of the crowd and continue to stay at the lower rungs of the success ladder? And, why only *the majority* of people always see illness even in their best wellness?

The Key Answers: In the process of *courageously combating the countless odds that continuously confront* them, those very few - *the minuscule minority* - the leaders with grit and determination and the focus of an eagle, keep fighting; keep on fighting the life's worst battles with all their might, till they finally emerge as the winners, placing themselves one notch above the others on the life's pedestal, clearly and boldly standing separate from the chicken-hearted *majority*. More often, the majority of people, maybe comprising over 95% of the human race, are not so well prepared to meet life's consequences with such dexterity that they remain at the lowest rungs of the success ladder, struggling, struggling, and forever struggling, timidly submitting to the circumstances, *brazenly binding their bizarre behavior* to some insipid thing called *FATE*!!

The former few of the people, who comprise the minuscule minority, *are amazingly and admiringly accustomed to always* see wellness even in their worst illness. They are the people with a tough mental frame and an unyielding attitude and consist of those who always stand apart from the crowd. On the other hand, majority of the people forming bulk of the human race, are so timorous that they forever prefer to remain locked up in their soiled frames of minds and are tuned to always see the worst illness even in their best wellness! And the startling fact is, you are always simultaneously surrounded by these two categories of people wherever you are; and of course, by the majority always in majority, and by the minority, always in minority!

The Introspection: Now, having said about the people you are surrounded by, let me make a straightforward attempt to know which class of people you represent and group with - the minuscule minority with that nerve of steel, or the vast majority with that low morale and mental fiber. Upon introspection, if you indeed notice that you are already in the astounding bracket of the very small segment of the people from the former category, who are exceptionally bestowed with the *power of proven prudence that places them in the list of the pacesetters*, then you have every reason to feel excited about. Because, you are already in the driver's seat, taking good control of the situation you are in, and not allowing yourself to get drifted away to an altogether *unknown, unfamiliar, unidentified, and unwanted* no man's land!

Conversely, if you do notice that you constitute the inopportune band of the oversized section of the people from the latter category, who cannot decide for themselves, prefer to remain as motionless passengers seated like pumpkins, refusing to shift to the driver's seat, *willingly willing to get their valuable means washed away*, then it's absolutely the time you started taking notice of the loud ringing of the warning bells!!

You need to instantly sit up and take stock of the situation since you are courageous enough to bracket yourself within the category of the majority of people who have no guts and fortitude to create their own lives and who always prefer to be dependent rather than dependable! It's time you made the necessary self-corrections urgently.

Now, the big question: How to analyze boldly and truthfully which group you are into, without giving scope for any bias in your own judgment about yourself? Let me elaborate here a little further. To say the least, how can you deliver any biased judgment in favour of yourself in the first place, especially when you are in the decision-making seat?

In normal circumstances, when the people at stake are your own kith and kin and even though your judgment about them is impartial, yet there may be allegations that you are biased in your pronouncement. But here the situation is different. You yourself are the decision-maker and you are also simultaneously the same person on whom your decisions are solely applied; then, how is it possible that you will be biased?

The answer is amazingly simple. Your self-interests are much at stake here. Since you must assess yourself threadbare being in the decision-making seat, you tend to go soft about yourself! In the process, you have the propensity to ignore your shortcomings and rate yourself higher than what you are, leading to the emergence of a well-biased judgment in favour of yourself! In contrast, when you have to decide for others, you have the propensity to ignore their strengths and rate them lower than what they actually are! *The point here is, while you are biased against others, you are biased in favour of yourself too. However, the big difference is, while you outrightly and with a prejudiced mind put others down by being biased against them, you put yourself undeservingly up by being biased in favour of you!* In the process, you always find yourself right even though the entire world stamps you *wrong...AND,* you keep on blatantly branding the world wrong, despite well knowing that the world is *right!*

Tendency to refuse to accept the truth: You, constituting the most 'intelligent' race called 'mankind' on this planet, have the instinctive tendency to refuse to accept the truth about yourself and your glaring shortcomings. In the garb of your so-called intelligence (not wisdom, mind you!), you always tend to become a *faultfinder* rather than a *factfinder*. Let us suppose, you have a wonderful team working for you to evaluate the genuine performance of others. You tend to un-see and un-acknowledge the unbiased and authentic effort that has been demonstrated by your functional team especially while assessing the performance of those who have fallen from your grace and whom the team has rated extremely high on the integrity scale. You lose the grace to even acknowledge the genuine efforts made by your own team for its true findings, since the persons in question, about whom your own team has reported favourably, are not in your good books. Your this *'super ability'* to put people down increases many folds especially when it comes to others whom you do not like, and when their legitimate interests are at stake. However, your opinion vastly varies when it comes to you or your own people. Why this discrimination? Because you do not have the courage to accept the truth about yourself and your shortcomings.

What do you get by truthfully analyzing yourself? Three things instantly happen when you truthfully analyze yourself. *First and foremost:* You start accepting the truth about yourself, however tart it sounds and looks. *Second and subsequent:* You start looking into the mirror opposite you to find the life-size inhuman human glaring at you, mocking at your *'glories'*, forcing you to make a quick rewind of the life of grandeur you *lived* till then. *Third and consequent:* You start accepting your shortcomings, however bitter and unending they may appear. When these three things happen, by default comes the stupendous change in you...not to be and no more to be biased in favour of you, even when your major interests are at stake. *Effect?* You start making self-corrections paving the way for the creation of an aura around you that puts you on the diving board, from where you can take an unfathomable plunge into the deepest ocean of profound conscience toward life's *varied, vivid, and wondrous* state, a condition essential for you to perform in an honest and transparent way so as to bring in clarity in whatever you think, express and act upon.

Having thus found the new theme, which is effervescent and full of life, you now will be in an *unbiased* position with an *unbiased* mind to assess yourself in an *unbiased* manner. Now the task of assessing your own credentials becomes stress-free and you can easily and honestly categorize yourself into one of the two groups...i). the eagle-focused minuscule minority eager to work not only for itself but for the betterment of the society as a whole, i. e., the zealous lot bubbling with enthusiasm comprising people who are bequeathed with the golden attitude to only see *wellness even in their worst illness, OR,* ii). the chicken-hearted vast majority always running away from its responsibilities, refusing to shoulder any task that is assigned to it under one pretext or the other, in the process always reining-in itself to the threshold of *doom, disease, and destruction,* hopelessly endangering itself with the many perils of life, unable to safeguard not only itself from the damage and infinite harm it is causing to itself but to the society as a whole, i. e., the depressed lot comprising people who are ordained to see only *illness even in their best wellness.*

It's Ultimately Your Choice: Now the moot question is, which category of people do you wish to *finally* associate, grow with, and become? *That category that always sees wellness even in its worst illness, OR that category, which always sees only illness even in its best wellness?* The tip to help you to land at the apt answer to this important question is, *"the choice is yours"* since the issue concerns you.

In order to arrive at the apt answer to the above question, you have to pick up the right choice from a series of choices available in front of you. The different situations that confront you from which you can pick your choice are indeed many. To quote a few: Whether to reduce to rubble your otherwise blissful life with trivial and insignificant issues or to light up your already troubled life by espousing the right attitude that empowers you with the discretion about what to seize and what to raze, is your choice. Whether to make or break your life, is your choice. Whether to win or lose life's battles, is your choice. Whether to become panicky or remain calm in challenging situations, is your choice. Whether to look up with hope and confidence in order to find steady solutions to your tribulations or to look down and surrender in tough times, is your choice. Whether to cultivate a tough mind in order to face the tough times, or to bow down and succumb to pressures, is your choice. Finally, whether to lead a *life with life* or, a *life without life,* is your choice...

Out of the many choices thus available to you, the choice to pick the right choice or the wrong choice is absolutely again your choice! However, you need to well keep in mind that, you pick invariably the right choice that makes you strong in mind and supple at heart so that the real human, already residing inside you, and bestowed with the ability to see only wellness in any illness is born! The transformation of you into this kind of human being is the need of the hour. In line with the adage *as the going gets tough the tough get going,* the completely transformed human inside you, taking the shape of a tough human, will have the courage to first see wellness in any illness and then bring wellness into that illness!!

Is it enough to bring the transformation only within you? The answer is clearly a big *NO.* You also need to honestly chip in your time and energy to the extent possible to bring the required cheer to all those who are always at the receiving end of life and are forced to lead a condemned *life without life* for no fault of theirs. You need to elevate the lives of such distressed/underprivileged too and bring them at par with you. How can you ensure this? By developing the zeal for the greatest asset of mankind, called humanity. Who can do this? Those people, who keep their nerve together even when death is staring at them; those people, who will not allow their measured smiles to vanish from their lips even when they are in a scorching embrace with the worst predicament of their lives; and those people, the very limited reserve of the mankind who, with their insurmountable approach towards life, defeat the life's hardships at every turn. In order to provide the much-needed relief to the people in distress, the sick, and the downtrodden, all these people, the prized lot, will rise to the occasion by selflessly displaying their zeal for humanity. Do you comprise this prized lot?

However, before answering the above question, it is necessary to know who decides who the distressed/underprivileged are. Is it you? If yes, then what is the yardstick? Materialistic comforts? or, the imperceptible, self-centered, and haughty intelligence levels? If yes, then what is the reference point to start with? If you consider your current level in both these areas as the reference point and then start making the measurement in terms of the above two yardsticks, then your exercise is bound to be erratic. Because you tend to brand whoever falls below the level you are currently in, as distressed/underprivileged. By so doing, can you forget that several people already enjoying a much higher position than you in reference to your current position in the above two areas, by the same yardstick and logic, may also brand you as distressed/under-privileged, though you may in fact be enjoying a privileged rank till then by virtue of your own position? This makes it clear that these two are not the real yardsticks to measure a person's authentic value. Then, what is the real yardstick?

The Real Yardstick: The real yardstick is your intrinsic ability to see *wellness even in the worst illness* and to develop the right attitude required for this. You will be able to do this only when you first stop thinking and acting from your own point of view and start thinking and acting from the other person's point of view, both times, of course, in an unbiased manner! You must possess the fundamental ability to differentiate between proper and improper, fair, and unfair, and right and wrong. Once you develop these qualities, you would automatically be equipped with the real yardstick by which you can measure the real state of life of people around you in an unbiased manner, paving the way for initiating the right course of action to bring in cheers into the lives of them as well. Your exercise then becomes scientific being bereft of any bias.

By appreciating the veracity of the statement *attitude, but not aptitude, determines one's altitude,* you know that the success in your life is not due to your aptitude, i. e., the so-called insensitive intelligence, but only due to your attitude, i. e., the approach towards life and people. So, do you have the right attitude so that you will always see Wellness even in your worst Illness? Or are you always seeing the worst Illness even in your best Wellness in view of your wrong attitude? Do you honestly figure in the same class of the people who fit into the former definition? Do you see the true and celebrated human living inside you? Or do you find that the true and celebrated human already living inside you is leaving you? You need to peep inside you and answer with an unbiased mind since the issue concerns you.

It's time to take this important decision NOW, and simultaneously act upon it by putting your heart and soul into it! Are You Ready To Do So?

--//--

Crime And Corruption

3

Preamble: The word *Crime* has many connotations, the important ones being:

a. an act committed in violation of law where the consequence of conviction by a court is punishment, especially where the punishment is a serious one such as imprisonment

b. an unlawful activity, a serious offense, especially in violation of morality, and

c. an unjust, senseless, or disgraceful act or condition

When it comes to the word ***Corruption***, the word also has many tones, viz.,

a. the act of corrupting or state of being corrupt

b. moral perversion; depravity

c. dishonesty, especially, bribery

d. putrefaction or decay

e. perversion of integrity

f. corrupt or dishonest proceedings

g. debasement or alteration, as of a language or a text or a word

h. any corrupting influence or agency

The root cause of Corruption: On a careful examination of the many meanings cited above, which have been sourced from the ever-dependable Concise Oxford Dictionary, ultimately it may be apt to say that the word corruption denotes impairment of *virtue* and *moral* *principles*, the two most important qualities one is expected to imbibe right from the time of one's childhood. In the present-day context of official dealings, corruption means inducement (as of a public official) by improper means (as bribery) to violate duty (as by committing a felony), which is the offshoot of the decay of virtues and moral principles of the official in question.

If we honestly try to peruse what has been stated in the foregoing paragraph and try to establish the link that exists between virtue and moral principles on one hand, and corruption on the other, we can easily arrive at the logical conclusion. "Impairment of *virtue* and *moral principles* gives birth to *corruption*, which is undoubtedly a serious *crime*". This very clearly points out that where virtue and moral principles are absent, corruption is present, which further means, these two diametrically opposite states/situations simply cannot co-exist.

Overall, corruption in society is the summation of corruption in all its different manifestations. Be it physical corruption, mental corruption, moral corruption, fiscal corruption, literary corruption, judicial corruption, or, administrative corruption, etc., it eventually takes the form of systemic corruption, destroying the very basic fabric of the society, reducing it to ruins. The truth is, whatever form corruption takes, it ultimately becomes Frankenstein, in due course eliminating the very person who is the source of it. Whatever may be the different tones corruption takes, finally all those tones merge into one, ie., systemic corruption, as just stated above.

Definition of Society and its relevance in combating corruption: When we even casually see around us, we find that in the present-day scenario society is badly, sadly, and madly infected with corruption in more ways than one. Before proceeding further, I find it important to define what society means. Again, taking recourse to the age-old and ever-dependable Concise Oxford Dictionary, society refers to the totality of people regarded as forming a community of *interdependent* individuals. It further connotes a group of people broadly distinguished from other groups by *mutual* interests, participation in *characteristic* relationships, *shared* institutions, and a *common* culture, such as a *rural society* and a *literary society*, etc. It also means an organization or association of persons engaged in a conspicuously common profession, activity, or interest, such as *a folklore society* or *a society of birdwatchers, a society of chain smokers*, etc.

What is very interesting in the definition given for the word society is, it's finally the congregation of *interdependent* individuals through which one *common* thread passes distinctly setting them apart from others in qualities and interests. As the adage *birds of the same feather flock together* befittingly suggests, people with common interests, cultures, habits, etc., group together and comprise individual societies. That's why we have societies/organizations distinctly differentiated with distinct characteristics that distinctly set them apart. And precisely this is the reason, why and how we often come across societies/organizations/ departments which are en masse known for their collective image... as very clean, very corrupt, very responsive, very aggressive, very responsible, very efficient, very lethargic, very casual, etc. The qualities with which a society/organization is known for are reflected in the working of the society/organization as a whole, since the individuals who comprise that society/organization are interdependent on each other and share common values/interests/habits that may make or break the image of the society/organization they represent.

When the core values of a society or an organization are not sustained in the long run, be it due to the exodus of its law-abiding people or an influx of law-evading people, no time will be lost to brand that particular society or organization decadent, putting a big question mark on the society's or organization's right to continue its existence or business any further. As we all know, wherever the individuals who comprise an organization are law-abiding and uphold the core values, that organization shall radiate with enthusiasm, delivering its best, in the process building and earning people's trust. The opposite is also equally true, where even one single individual starts unwinding the spiral of values, slowly setting in the vicious process of unfurling corrupt practices, in view of its devastating cascading effect, its evil tentacles will spread to every nook and corner of the organization, in no time bringing down its image to nadir.

How to ensure a Corruption-free Society/Organization? Ensuring a corruption-free society/organization is a two-fold process. First, build the society/organization with clean people with impeccable and spotless character, loaded with virtues and moral principles. Then, bar the entry of any individual with a proven track record of shady deals, so as to ensure the continuance of its spot-less image. As we all know, a single rotten apple will spoil the barrel of good apples. Don't allow the rotten apple to enter the barrel of good apples!

Now the next point is, how to set in the process of cleansing any entity that is already found infected with corrupt people, corrupt practices, and corrupt approaches. I.e., how to cleanse the barrel that already has rotten apples? The answer is age-old and very simple...again this is also the same two-fold process as just stated; first, ruthlessly remove the rotten apples, one by one, from the barrel and throw them away, however unassuming they may look from outside. Then, start replacing the rotten apples with good ones. I.e., first, show the doors to the law-evading and simultaneously open the doors to the law-abiding. Though this process may be comparatively difficult, it definitely is not impossible if we have the necessary tenacity and fortitude to do it.

Eventually, in order to make the society/organization corruption-free, thereby crime-free, it is essential that the core human values of honesty and transparency comprising virtues and moral principles are steadily built into its rank and file, in a systematic, honest, and transparent way. It may be very apt to quote the late Dr. A.P.J. Abdul Kalam here in the context of these two finest human qualities, which are necessary to ensure a corruption-free and thereby a crime-free society/organization. In Chapter 7 (*Getting the Forces Together*) of one of his widely read books, *"Ignited Minds: Unleashing the Power within India"*, Dr. Kalam recalls his interaction with Sumitra Kulkarni, the granddaughter of the Mahatma, in respect of honesty in public life. The incident as it happened, in Dr. Kalam's own words:

Quote:

"The subject of transparency and values brings to my mind Gandhiji. I happened to meet in Delhi his granddaughter, Sumitra Kulkarni. I asked her, Sumitraji, is there a particular incident (in respect of honesty in public life) that you always remember from your grandfather's life?

She narrated to me this story... Every day, as you all would have heard, Mahatma Gandhi held a prayer meeting at a fixed time in the evening. After the prayers, there would be a collection of voluntary gifts for the welfare of Harijans and others. The devotees of Gandhiji used to collect whatever was given by the people of all sections and this collection was counted by a few members suggested by Gandhiji. The amount so collected would be informed to Gandhiji before dinner. The next day, a man from the bank would come to collect the money for deposit.

Once the man reported that there was a shortage of a few paise in the money handed over to him and the amount informed to Gandhiji the previous night. Gandhiji, on hearing this, was so upset that he went on fast saying that this is a poor man's donation, and we have no business to lose any of it."

After narrating the above incident, Dr. Kalam says:

"This episode is a unique example of transparency in public life. Well, in the same country we are witnessing the best and the worst. We should all, particularly the young generation, launch a movement for a transparent India, just as our fathers fought for our freedom. Transparency is a cornerstone of development."

Unquote:

Need of the Hour: The value, values play in our daily lives in ensuring a corruption-free society/organization, thereby a crime-free society/organization, can well be understood from the above highly exhilarating incident quoted by Dr. Kalam. The wheel is already invented. You need not re-invent the wheel.

You simply have to put into practice and duplicate, what the great sons & daughters of this great soil have long back done and practiced and preached us to practice, for the betterment of society. You need to listen to your inner voice and act accordingly, before closing any deal. The need of the hour hence is to build a cadre of value-based citizens, who possess the guts to flush out the evil of corruption from public life. The need of the hour is to show the doors to the law-evading and open the doors to the law-abiding. You need to become a part of this great exercise.

It's time to take this important decision NOW, and simultaneously act upon it by putting your heart and soul into it! Are You Ready To Do So?

--//--

4

Policy Never Above Humanity

The word Policy has got its origins in the Latin word *'politia'*, meaning administration. In General English, the word means a plan or course of action, as of a government, political party, or business, intended to influence and determine decisions, actions, and other matters (*as, India's foreign policy, the company's personnel policy, the government's controversial economic policy"* etc). It further means "a *course of action, guiding principle* or *procedure* considered *expedient, prudent or advantageous*".

Before proceeding further, it may be necessary to understand why at all a policy is needed to be framed in the first place. Can't we do without Policies? Let me hasten to add here that the word "Policy" in the present context has nothing to do with the term in reference to the Insurance we buy, where it broadly means 'contract'. A detailed definition in the present context describes a policy *as a set of principles, rules, and guidelines formulated or adopted by an Organization/State to reach its long-term goals and typically published in a booklet or other form that is widely accessible.* Policies impose serious restrictions; all activities must take place within the boundaries set by them. Along with procedures, policies ensure that the point of view held by the governing body, or an organization is translated into steps that result in an outcome compatible with that view. That's why, at the organizational, State, or National level, the need for framing a Policy has become so important.

Hereinafter, wherever the word 'policy' occurs in this article, the word equally means a Circular, an Office Memorandum, Guidelines, Rules, etc., which are generally issued by an organization/office from time to time intended to improvise different services/facilities or in the context of introducing certain changes in the functioning of the organization/office.

Having said so about the need and necessity that lie behind the framing of a Policy, it is indeed a misfortune that the people down below, who are the implementers of various policies, during different stages of policy implementation, instead of un-framing the 'framed' policy and ensuring its implementation in totality so that the objective with which the said policy has been framed reaches out to the beneficiaries, are in fact, making 'certain' that the policy forcibly remains tight in its 'tight' frames. Thus, laid to 'rest', the policy continues to remain in the locked-up cupboards, gathering dust, resulting in the targeted beneficiaries not being able to benefit from the fruits the policy would have otherwise delivered. Its wings having thus been clipped to the base, the bird of policy, instead of flying high and spreading the aroma of its benefits, is getting confined to the dark corporate/bureaucratic labyrinth, from where it can never see the light of the day. And these policies, surviving the test of time by 'gathering dust' through the ages and miserably failing to deliver the goods, are obviously no better than the deceased.

This is the story of the countless policies that suffered a dreadful rot at the hands of the conservative and conformist few over many years, who are always opposed to the idea of the benefits of the policy reaching out to the larger number of people they were intended for. This is more so the case, particularly in Public Sector Organizations/Govt offices. As time passes, a new policy takes birth at regular intervals, intended either to replace or supplement the earlier one, either at a company, State, or National level, only to see its quick demise at its infancy itself as a toddler due to opposition by a section of the public, thus ceasing to exist even before learning how to stand, let alone fly. The commonality, however, between these two types of policies (the former ones- living a very long life 'surviving' the test of time by gathering dust in the locked-up cupboards, and the later ones - meeting their ill-fated demise right at their infancy), nevertheless is the same...failing to serve the purpose which they were meant for!

While the above is the fate of the numerous policies the man with concern for his fellow man has made, there is nonetheless an iota of doubt that quite a few of them have virtually brought smiles on the wrinkled faces of the subjugated and the oppressed, unfolding innumerable benefits to them. However, the ploy remains here... While the so-called benefits reach only a microscopic section of the people, a vast section of the people are still deprived of and denied the fruits, under one pretext or the other. A few 'learned' implementers of the policy, possessing very 'high skills' of reading the policy between the lines (where nothing is written, the space is blank and you and I cannot see anything), in the name of so-called interpretation of the complex language used in the policy, somehow strive to conclude how and why the 'provisions' of the policy come in the way of their total implementation and how and why its benefits cannot be extended to a particular section of the people. However, the misfortune here is, 'that' particular section of the people also comprises the list of beneficiaries of the policy in question.

During the course of running the affairs of the State or an organization, the policymakers, while drafting a 'policy', insert many sections, and sub-sections into it. These sub-sections in particular, are invariably interspersed with such supercilious language that they either cannot be easily interpreted, and if yes, can be interpreted in many ways by many people, or can have very long and baffling interpretations that no common person can understand! Further, the content of certain sections/sub-sections may hint at the imposition of unwanted restrictions on the continuation of certain genuine benefits which were till then available to the people, or unjustly curtail their freedom in some way or the other, or altogether bring in a new state of situation that is diametrically opposed to the existing one suppressing the humanitarian needs of the people, resulting in the said policy causing a possible breach of trust existing till then between the policymakers and the public, leading to unleashing of protest. Precisely it is here, where the tenet *"Policy Never Above Humanity"* comes to play...

During the course of implementation of a policy, if it is indeed noticed that even a single section/sub-section of the policy is coming in the way of extending the benefits to the people whom the policy is intended for, then that offending section/sub-section is ought to be altogether obliterated from the text of the policy, not to speak about the action required to be taken when a new policy is opposed in toto. For, as just said, as the policy is never above humanity, no rule, no section of the Law, or no chapter of an Act, can in effect be allowed to contain any oppressive content, that unjustly comes in the way of its full and total implementation for the larger benefits of the people it is intended for; else, the very purpose of its framing ever stands unrealized.

Similarly, if lack of content, and/or clarity is resulting in the denial of its benefits to the beneficiaries, in that case also, the policymakers are equally responsible to bring in quick and clear amendments to the policy, so that again the larger objective lying behind its framing is not defeated and the unjust denial of its benefits to the deserving does not happen. The withdrawal of the three farm laws by the Central Govt in Dec'21, though a couple of years after their enactment, is a fit case in point that shall be remembered in the annals of the history of the country as a measure taken genuinely bowing to the wishes of the protesting farmers.

Here it may be apt to quote from Dr. APJ Abdul Kalam's *"A Manifesto for Change"*, which is the result of Dr. Kalam's five years of research on the Parliamentary System of India, and which is a sequel to his earlier book *"India 2020"*, published in 1998, that was amazingly ahead of its times... The vision Dr. Kalam presented in this magnificent book went on to inspire directly or indirectly many sectors of the economy to work for and achieve high growth. In *"A Manifesto for Change"*, while throwing brilliant light on the Inclusive Governance for sustainable development, and in the context of framing policies, Dr. Kalam says:

Quote:

It is the government's job to bring smiles to the faces of a billion people by enacting appropriate policies and laws and facilitating societal transformation. We have been working with policies and procedures that are mostly based on mistrust. These led to the framing of extractive policies in almost all departments.

Underlying the policies was a control mindset instead of a facilitating mindset. This dampened the motivation and empowerment at all levels of governance in productive sectors and among the people. The irony is that Indians have shown enormous resilience and achieved phenomenal success when provided with an environment of trust and confidence in the working space."

Unquote:

Have we ever tried to introspect whether our policies/rules are based on mistrust or trust? Whether our policies are extractive in nature or inclusive and for growth? Whether we frame our policies with a control mindset or a facilitating mindset? If our policies/rules are based on mistrust, extractive in nature, and are framed with a control mindset, then it's high time we rethought on our policy of policy framing and relooked at the rudiments that are necessary to be taken into consideration before we embark on working on yet another policy! Otherwise, our policies, which continue to take birth at regular intervals as said in the beginning, will either remain confined to the rusted cupboards and die a death due to suffocation, or destined to die a pre-mature death, due to public displeasure...

Now the question is, can we afford to have a policy based on mistrust? Trust is the very pillar on which a robust policy framework rests. When policies are interlaced with the fine threads of trust, they live their life, fulfilling the needs of all the sections of society. On the other hand, if the threads of trust are intertwined, or worst, replaced with the threads of mistrust, the canvas of policy gets peeled off quickly, losing its original sheen and briskness, in the process totally failing to serve the purpose for which it has originally been woven. Can we have the right to run the administration, if our policies/rules are branded anti-people and anti-worker? Don't we have the responsibility to rise to the occasion and wipe out many a tear from the face of those oppressed, depressed, and suppressed lot and bring cheers into their troubled lives?

Having a genuine concern for the people who are downtrodden, brow-beaten, and exploited is a great quality. But is it enough to just have a genuine concern? Is it not necessary that the so-called genuine concern is translated into a sincere action aimed at transforming the lives of those who deserved it for the better, forever? While framing our policies, are we at least first trying to ensure that we are addressing the core issues that are positioning themselves like erect concrete blocks between the policies and the beneficiaries? Looking at what is happening around us, at the workplace, and in the marketplace, we can't claim that we are properly addressing all the issues, before framing a policy...Can we?

Before framing a policy, it's customary that a draft policy is first released facilitating the study of its contents by the think tank of the people. Views of the stakeholders are solicited on the existence of lacunae or unfair content in the draft document if any, with the assurance that the said lacunae or unfair content shall be appropriately addressed in the final document! But in practice, in how many cases the public-review is accorded its due?

Though the concerned section of the society takes the herculean pains of reading the draft document line by line and sends its views to the framers, nothing suggested finds a place in the final policy document and the initial draft document comes out as it is, as the final policy document too. The reason oft cited for this insensitive action is that no constructive views were received. Then, doesn't it make sense that the draft policy itself is framed with absolute care and with due regard to the welfare of the targeted section of society? What is the final solution?

Simple...The policy needs to be framed *NOT* with a control mindset, but with a facilitating mindset. The policy needs to be framed *NOT* based on mistrust, but on trust. The policy needs to be *NOT* extractive, but inclusive in nature. The policy needs to be framed without any bias, whatsoever. Only then, we can bring smiles to the faces of the over a billion Indians as very rightly stated by Dr. A.P.J. By doing this only we can bring in the required societal transformation as opined by our respected late former President, since as the title of this article *'policy never above humanity'* says, everything else comes only after the humanitarian requirements of the people are fully and genuinely met with. We need to invariably think, pause, and then embark on our efforts before we ink our next draft policy if we are really serious to ensure that all the benefits of that next policy reach all the beneficiaries without exception.

Before going aboard to draft an altogether new policy, or to draft amendments as a sequel to an existing one, it is hence absolutely necessary that the existing policies are suitably amended first by clipping the absurdities and oppressive content they contain so that they become more relevant, realistic and people friendly.

We should have a natural mechanism by which our existing policies undergo a regular review, say every two-three years, to ensure that they don't become objects of ridicule but get defined and re-defined and stay updated and remain in sync with the changing times/needs. This caring task, of course, is highly herculean, but definitely not impossible.

As the adage *Charity begins at Home* goes, there is an urgent need to at least bring this refreshing change first within the organization/workplace one is in. And no change is possible without the active and genuine involvement of the people. For this to happen, you need to first become the torch bearer in your organization/office.

It's time to take this important decision NOW, and simultaneously act upon it by putting your heart and soul into it! Are You Ready To Do So?

--//--

5

Managers Vs Damagers

The other day, I was talking to a grand old man robed in majestic native Rajasthani attire in the vast corridors of the Amber Palace (also known as the Amer Palace/Fort) in Rajasthan during our trip to that princely state during the winter of 2015. After a rather lengthy yet very thoughtful conversation, I was delighted to know that, that 'young' gentleman had already encircled the Sun 88 times. He was very enthusiastic and well-conversant with the state of affairs of our blessed country. However, I did notice a dash of disenchantment in his otherwise vibrant voice whenever the conversation took a turn toward the administrative and technical strengths our country is possessing in the field of governance.

"Quite a few of the current schemes of the Government are still not system-driven despite the fact that the country has witnessed rapid strides, particularly in the fields of IT services and communications", the gentleman in his late '80s had briskly opened up in chaste English. "We must be phenomenally proud of the people who are responsible for the commendable rise seen in these two fields", the grand old man had continued. "Fortunately, they are not like most of the typical Managers of today's Public Sector, but are clear dreamers, who are really hungry about the country's growth", the clear voice of the man with the pristine look had further endured. "Today's typical Managers, more so in the Public Sector, are rather like 'Damagers' of the systems, so painstakingly built by the visionaries of the yesteryears", the versatile super senior citizen had summed up, this time his voice sounding rather unforgiving.

His contemptuous concluding observation that *"today's typical Managers, more so in the Public Sector, are rather like 'Damagers' of the systems"*, had upset me to the core, and forced me to introspect, for I was also a product of a Public Sector Organization (the Maharatna coal behemoth, Coal India Ltd), then working in one of its subsidiaries, Western Coalfields Ltd., headquartered at Nagpur.

The word "Damagers" sounded very thought-provoking as it not only perfectly rhymed with the word "Managers" but felt to be a complete contra to it in meaning. Does the humble word (heard by me for the first time) simply mean persons who cause damage to someone or something, or those who derail/sabotage the well-laid-out systems? A quick reference to a couple of authoritative lexicons of the English language did not yield any result either, as the singular noun of the word couldn't be found in either of them. A subsequent online search had lent some credibility to the initial guess, and I couldn't stay without admiring the imposing gentleman for having 'invented' an altogether new word in the English language and introducing me to it! Mountain of gratitude to him, as but for him, I couldn't have coined the scintillating title for this article I was contemplating to write for some time on the theme that centres around managerial positioning, its positive/ negative shades, steps involved in the transformation of an employee from being a 'damager' to becoming a manager and beyond, and the various connotations that surround the whole process!

The crisp observation of the grand octogenarian had given rise to the birth of the following revelations in me with respect to the working of a Public Sector Organization in today's energetic era where cut-throat competition is ruling the roost, leaving no choice before an organization but to perform in order to survive. Otherwise, no time would be lost for the organization to perish. Here go my revelations...

    i. *Visibility of a clear mismatch between the 'growth' of an organization as perceived from outside and that actually seen from inside: A clear mismatch is conspicuously visible between the 'growth' of a Public Sector Organization as perceived from outside, and the real growth of the organization actually 'seen' from inside and 'felt' within. The growth of an organization might be measured in reference to several parameters; however, there are three most important parameters, the growth in which distinctly decides the decisive growth of an organization. These are: first and foremost, the technical competence possessed by its workforce, then its financial performance, and then its public image, in that order. Out of these three, the first parameter, technical competence, forms the pedestal on which the second parameter, financial performance is built, which in turn facilitates the rise in its third parameter, public image. If an organization flounders on the first two parameters, its third parameter, public image, obviously suffers the biggest dent. While the second and third parameters, viz., financial performance and public image can be compared to the mantle and crust of the earth respectively, the first parameter, technical competence, can be compared to the core of the earth. By technical competence I mean the in-depth capability of studying, understanding, imbibing, and finally adapting the core competencies by the total workforce of the organization combined with a great customer-centric attitude and outstanding administrative competence coupled with red hot focus on delivery of the product/ service in the quality promised, and introduction of cutting-edge technologies into the organization which will help the organization to stand up and compete at the global level.*

ii. **Visibility of parochially procedure-centric work culture:** *This outlandishly downbeat procedure-centric rather than performance-centric environment present in a public sector organization is consistently promoted by those who have vested interests in the continuity of the human element (heavily loaded with wrong intentions) in matters where a system-driven environment can effortlessly takeover.*

iii. **Movement of the strategic decision-making process over rough terrain:** *The decision-making process is seldom smooth and is somehow 'pulled' from the front and 'pushed' from the rear and is* *'guided' by a batch of hired and tired individuals with no trace of fire in their bellies, and who are not in a hurry to sizzle up the organization.*

iv. ***Absence of commitment and gut feeling:*** *These two vital elements primarily responsible for an organization's fortifying performance are often not decisively displayed by the organization's top brass, severely affecting the organization's performance during troubled times. By gut feeling I mean the ability to quickly decide what is good and what is not for the accelerated growth of the organization, the wisdom to differentiate between these two, and the courage to prop the good and drop the bad.*

v. ***Absence of transparency in the day-to-day working:*** *People at higher levels usually talk in hushed tones. The higher the hierarchy, the more hush-hush the tone becomes. Unfortunately, the malady percolates down the hierarchy at a rapid speed, crippling the efficient functioning of the organization. Inherent resistance to discuss various shortcomings is quite often prominently visible even amongst the rank and file of the organization.*

vi. ***Absence of accountability:*** *No fear for failure to deliver what is promised, and prevalence of tendency to put the blame squarely on others and sometimes even on the environment, for the said failure.*

vii. ***Prevalence of the attitude of 'what-I-do-is-always-right':*** *Convincing oneself that whatever is done is not only the right option but the only option available in the given circumstances and that no further improvement can be brought in, i.e., refusal to:*

    a. *critically examine what has been done*

    b. *honestly accept the shortcomings, and own up the responsibilities, and*

    c. *initiate corrective measures even if it is indeed noticed that what had been done earlier was not in the right interest of the organization.*

viii. ***Reluctance to Raise the Bar for oneself:*** *Employees right from the section-head level continually raise the bar for others in the structure, but not for themselves, i.e., having increasing expectations and demanding improvement from others, but never from themselves.*

ix. ***Vulnerability to influences:*** *Many employees at every level demand favours from those within as well as outside the organization and harbor the wretched inability to resist such sordid temptations.*

x. ***Presence of a severe dent in the moral and ethical fabric of the organization:*** *Many employees at every level lack ethics and values. Worse, they propagate the practice of the highest order of living and leading at every available opportunity and from every available platform, but rarely practice the same themselves.*

All the revelations made above, though per se were in reference to a Public Sector Organization in general, are equally applicable to the private sector, as well as all the departments/offices of Central, State & UT Governments too. Needless to say, refreshingly there may be certain vivid exceptions too in the Public & Private Sector Organizations and different Government offices where the flaws pointed out above may be completely absent! The revelations hold substantial validity at the individual level also, which means, we as individuals are destined to perish **IF** we fail, or worse, refuse to perform.

Hereinafter in the text, wherever a reference is made to one gender, it equally applies to the other gender as well.

With a view to arriving at a possible solution so as to counter the resultant damage arising out of the flaws discussed, I have delved deeper into the nitty-gritty of the issue. Following are my observations with regard to putting a check on the continuity of the damage that has the devilish strength to cripple the overall functioning of an organization in the event the concerns expressed in the above revelations continue to happen even in a remote way...

A. The mismatch between the 'growth' of an organization visible from outside and that is actually prevalent inside, which perhaps forms the single most damaging element that spirals the other nine cited above, if indeed noticed, must be decisively stopped on day one itself, since an organization which is surviving on a 'borrowed shine' cannot continue its survival for long. Failure to quickly identify its unethical, and damaging individuals, who are instrumental in painting the 'silver coat' from outside, would prove very costly to the organization in the long run, and such individuals must be packed off at the earliest opportunity.

B. The more the mismatch, the more unequivocally it means that the organization's fundamentals are at serious stake, and this is a definite pointer to the fact that there is no real growth in what is known as the *TEN ASSENTING FACTORS* that unmistakably decide the position an organization takes in the corporate world.

These formidable factors, already interspersed in the revelations listed above, can further be crisped, and categorized as below:

1. technical/administrative competence and strategic decision-making ability

2. willingness to effectively implement the decisions taken

3. willingness to implement a system-centric culture

4. commitment and gut feeling

5. absolute transparency

6. courage not to blame others and the environment for failures at the individual level

7. commitment to:

   - deliver what is promised

   - keep up the time schedules in all activities whether customer or employee-oriented

   - critically examine what has been done

   - own up the shortcomings and

   - quickly unfold damage control measures

8. raising the bar first for himself and then for others around him when it comes to discharging the assigned duties/functions

9. commitment to oppose influences at the personal level, and finally

10. commitment to safeguarding the moral and ethical fabric of its entire human capital across the organization

The above ten assenting factors collectively comprise the single barometer on which every employee's overall credibility and performance are measured. Further, the effective discharge of one's duties and responsibilities squarely depends on the compliance of the above ten assenting factors. In the corporate hierarchy, while the focus migrates from bottom to top when it comes to shouldering & discharge of responsibilities, the reverse is just true in respect of the discharge of duties, where the focus migrates from top to bottom. While the CEO is required to shoulder and discharge several responsibilities and his performance is gauzed from the point of view of how successful he is at the discharge of his responsibilities, the employee at the bottom has little or no responsibilities, and his performance is gauzed from the point of view of how successful he is at the discharge of his duties. The following diagram depicts the above situation:

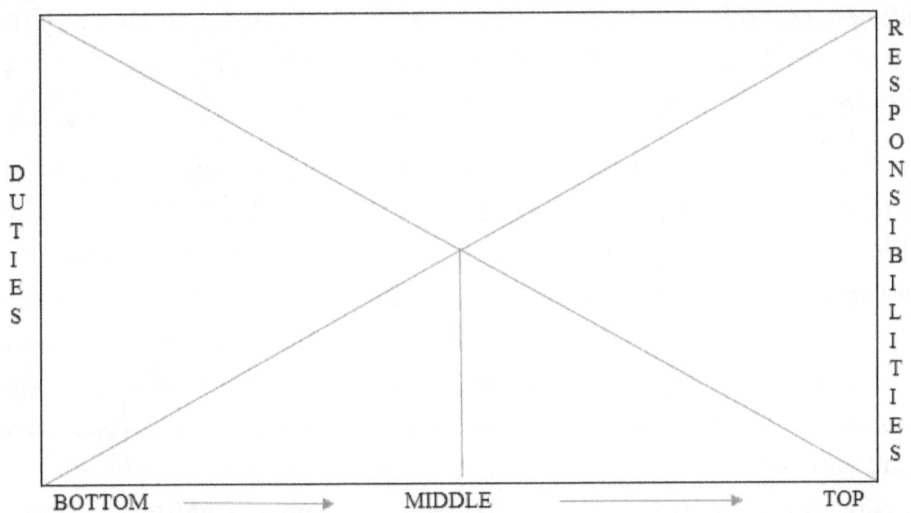

In the corporate journey from the bottom to top, responsibilities keep on increasing and duties keep on decreasing. It may further be observed from the above diagram that the employees at the middle level will have responsibilities and duties both in equal proportion. Irrespective of the level or position one is in, the degree of compliance of the ten assenting factors plays a very crucial role in fortifying one's level/position.

Hereinafter, it is essential to keep in mind that wherever the word 'Manager' appears in the text, it equally refers to each and every individual working in an organization, irrespective of the position one holds (right from the CEO to the employee at the rock-bottom level).

In order to ensure a healthy growth of the above ten assenting factors amongst all employees including the rank and file of an organization, we first need to know the content every single employee of an organization is made up of, and the intent he holds. By content, I again mean the technical/administrative competence/skill one possesses in his field of expertise/operations/activities, and by intent, I mean the thought process an individual cultivates, which also can be called the mindset, the attitude. It will be very interesting to notice from the above list that while the content part comprises only 10% of the list, i.e., just one single factor out of the ten (appearing at Sl. No.1 above), the intent part comprises the balance 90% of the list, i.e., the remaining nine assenting factors out of the ten!

In order to know their content and intent levels, the simple litmus test is to check where the employees stand on a scale of 1 to 10 (one being the lowest and ten being the highest) against each assenting factor outlined above. This test may be carried out in two ways; first, by the individuals themselves, ie., self-evaluation, in which all the employees would rate themselves on the scale. *However, while conducting self-evaluation, all employees need to be honest to the core.* Otherwise, their true self will not pop out and remains eclipsed by their own bias in favour of themselves. Second, by others, ie., peer-evaluation, in which all others in their respective departments/offices, irrespective of their position, would rate them on this scale.

How unbiased or biased an employee is about himself can be measured by comparison of these two scores, ie., the one arrived by self-evaluation and the other arrived by peer-evaluation. The less the gap between these two scores, the less biased he is about himself and vice versa. Nevertheless, the score arrived through peer evaluation would reflect the 'real' characteristics of an employee both inside and outside, and hence these scores would be considered as the concluding scores in the final assessment of the credentials of an employee.

Now about the test. In line with an organization's HR policy, the test may either be extended to the entire workforce, including its rank and file, or limited to a few levels, viz., from the middle level and above. While taking the test it must be borne in mind that the entire exercise is solely aimed at the betterment of each individual employee of the organization both at the professional and personal levels. As such it is highly essential that the exercise is carried out in strict confidence and hence the resultant data sourced from each and every employee must be kept highly confidential. It must be further remembered that every single employee of the organization who possesses a minimum experience of say, one year in the organization should be made eligible to participate in the exercise for peer evaluation. E.g., unless employee "A" has worked in the same department/section with employee "B" for a period of minimum one year, the opinion of employee "A" shall not be sought for evaluating the credentials of employee "B". After department-wise compilation of the self-evaluation and peer-evaluation scores of all the employees across the organization is complete, the said scores would be securely stored in the official data bank. Subsequently the entire data is carefully analysed by a special group assigned with the onerous responsibility.

Post completion of the final analysis by the special group, the performance level of each employee vis-à-vis the score he made on the above scale shall be arrived at as shown in the following table:

Score on the 10-point Scale based on Peer-Evaluation	Performance Level
Below 5	Damager
5 and above but below 8	Manager
8 and above but below 10	Leader
A clear 10 out of 10	Mentor

As can be seen from the above table, if an employee's peer-evaluation score is below 5, it means he is clearly a *Damager*. The minimum peer-evaluation scores of 5, 8, and 10 qualify one as a *Manager, Leader,* and *Mentor* respectively. As an illustration, if an employee's score is, say 7.2, it means that he is already a manager passing through the Manager-phase, and who is poised to become a Leader once his score becomes 8. Likewise, one can become a Mentor once he attains a score of 10. The above evaluation shall be carried out twice in a year and the level corresponding to the average of the two scores reflects the 'real' performance level of an employee during that particular year.

As stated in the above illustration, in the event an employee finds his score between 5 and 8 (say, again 7.2), by virtue of which he is already in the *Manager-phase*, it is the time when he should exercise utmost caution, for there may be testing circumstances that may influence his behaviour causing a slip by which he may quickly slide down on the scale and the reverse happens, bringing his score below 5, plunging him to the *Damager phase* from the creditable *Manager phase*. It may be pertinent to note that the reverse can happen at any stage and during any phase!

Similarly, though initially one finds himself scoring below 5 on the scale, by virtue of which he finds himself in the *Damager phase*, it may be possible that he improves upon his scores and climb up on the scale and graduate into the Manager, Leader, and Mentor phases over a period of time. The irony is, while the slip to the lower phases is quick and unnoticeably easy, the rise to the higher phases shall be slow and noticeably difficult! However, one thing is certain; one can decide for himself, where he wants to stay on the scale. The score one makes is the summation of the content and intent levels prevailing inside him. The surprising thing is, the score heavily depends on one's intent, ie., one's thought process or mind-set, which comprises 9 assenting factors, out of the 10, as already seen above!

While checking out an employee's overall score, it is highly essential that he scores at least 5 against each of the ten assenting factors, in order to claim that he is definitely at least a Manager, if not a Leader and a Mentor. A score of less than 5 against any single assenting factor will mean that he is a Damager in that particular area. In order to claim that overall, one is at least at the performance level of a Manager, he is required to simultaneously attain an aggregate score of a minimum of 50 against all the above ten assenting factors as well as a minimum score of 5 against each factor.

That means, an aggregate score of 50 and above, maybe 5 and above against nine factors but less than 5 against even one, will still label him as a "Damager" since he has not scored the minimum required 5 against one factor. A score of less than 5 against that single factor is enough to mar his overall credentials. This also shows the area(s) in which the employee in question needs improvement. The idea is, an employee must have a respectable score of 5 and above against all the 10 assenting factors, which means his credibility and competence must at least be above the halfway mark against all the factors. Once this is fulfilled, it indicates that the employee in question has achieved an acceptable all-round development, which is the core requirement necessary to get him recognized at least as a manager.

As a corollary, my earlier times while I was working in the Regional Sales Office of Coal India ltd in Chennai (from May 2000 to March 2012) came to my memory. During the close to 12 years I was in Chennai, on four occasions I got the opportunity to be a part of stunning seminars conducted by professionals from different fields on the HDI (Human Development Index) phenomenon and on how to secure a respectable HDI score at the individual as well as the organizational levels. Once I even had an opportunity to listen to a Nobel nominee in one such seminar, during the course of which, the speaker was categorizing the Managers working in both private as well as public sectors into two distinct groups as "performers" and "non-performers". According to the speaker, as per a nationwide survey once conducted, though performers as well as non-performers were noticed in both sectors, the percentage of non-performing managers in the public sector was always found to be unbelievably higher! Here Public Sector per se includes Government (Central, State, and UT) offices also. By not using the term "damagers" for describing the non-performers, did the speaker mean that the non-performing managers are perhaps less perilous than damagers, since 'no-action' any day is better than a 'damaging action'? As we know, the interests of the damagers are anytime detrimental to the interests of the organizations they are associated with, and thus are detrimental to the interests of the nation as well. In the wake of the connection that has emerged as above, I have made another attempt to analyze the reasons behind it and stumbled upon the following:

✓ *The foremost reason that immediately struck me was the general lack of accountability in the Public Sector's managers. Though a mechanism does exist in the Public Sector for pinning down responsibilities, however, due to its deplorably non-effective functioning, many of the managers get out of the charges of non-accountability with ease, leading to the adoption of a very casual approach by them towards several important and survival-deciding issues. Here survival refers to the survival of the organization!*

✓ *The second reason that struck me was the horrendous habit of passing on the buck down the line and making someone (usually the innocent lamb) the scapegoat, abashedly holding him responsible for the damage caused.*

✓ *Third, the usual practice of somehow 'managing' various issues/ assignments, instead of meeting them head-on and the resultant failure to arrive at clearly acceptable and long-term solutions (this aspect is further explained in detail, in the fifth reason stated below).*

✓ *Fourth, the sad practice of offering excuses rather than obvious reasons, when an important project gets delayed or something goes wrong, and the disinclination to analyze the failure. As we know, an obvious reason can be well analyzed rather than a lame excuse.*

✓ *Fifth, the frustrating convention of eulogizing someone for certain 'artificial' and quick 'gains' reported by him though having been fully aware that the action thus concluded was not in the long-term interests of the organization. I believe, when someone says and claims that he has somehow 'managed' a given task or a particular situation with 'great' difficulty, it only indicates that he has in fact, by some means, temporarily 'patched up' the assigned task but not accomplished it the way it was supposed to be accomplished. Somehow 'managing' an activity is no less than 'damaging' the activity...in the LONG RUN. This is the reason when an assigned task was 'somehow' carried out by the person to whom the task had been assigned, the 'gratitude' is conveyed by saying 'well managed', rather than by saying 'well done'. As we clearly see, there is a distinct difference between these two! Further, the relief received when an assigned task was 'somehow' managed, is always temporary!*

As a consequent lead, a strange phenomenon has caught my attention, which is attributed as a serious factor in paralyzing the functioning of an organization. The phenomenon is called the 'management-side' facet of functioning while dealing with certain critical issues of technical/administrative nature an organization encounters from the vigilance point of view, during the course of its business operations. The so-called 'strict' functioning of a 'management-side' functionary donning the mantle of a 'manager' while dealing with such issues cannot take the organization to any loftier heights. Because the approach of the 'management-side' functionary is more often bound by a mere formality, rather than clear practicality. The 'management-side' functionary, perhaps functioning as a self-designated 'saviour' of the organization, in fact, knowingly or unknowingly resorts to such steps during the course of his investigation, in view of which the organization's real interests may get seriously jeopardized. This particular situation predominantly holds true, when the management-side functionary is the one with a lack of foresight. When foresight is absent, the functioning of a 'management-side' functionary in an organization becomes lopsided and redundant, reducing his position from that of a "Manager" to a "Damager".

Another matter that causes concern is, while evaluating the efficiency and effectiveness of an individual, we tend to err by estimating his ability to deliver merely based on his so-called 'managerial' capability, ignoring the alerts of the day, and overlooking the damaging tales that cloud him. The Public Sector in general and as a consequence the nation as a whole, is already crumbling down under the enormous weight of such damaging Managers. As a natural upshot and as a matter of fact, managers should mature as leaders and mentors, over a period of time, as stated earlier. Unfortunately, this is not happening; worse, over a period of time, most managers, in fact, are stooping down to such low levels that they are putting their own interests in the forefront, pushing the interests of the organizations they represent to the farthest rear...

As we know, a manager who matured as a leader is the one who takes the right decisions at the right time, for the right reasons, and for the right people. In today's scenario, such managers who matured as leaders are rarely seen and may be available in a very limited number. On the contrary, whom we have in plenty are the damaging managers everywhere, who are known to be taking the wrong decisions, for the wrong reasons. Further, if at all a decision is taken, it is again in favour of the wrong people. Even worse, they take self-seeking decisions for self-seeking reasons. They are always found to be more prone to quick disreputable money, rather than steady reputable money and their ethics are always under question. They dejectedly ignore the fact that by doing so, they are in fact causing irreparable damage to their own reputation first, and as a consequence, to their families' reputation next, to their organizations' reputation in the third, and thereby finally to the reputation of the country in its entirety.

Leadership, as we know, comes only with unadulterated concern for the organization as a whole. The essential ingredient a leader must possess is the ability to provide ethical direction in testing times. Over the years, this impeccable quality gets quantified, layer by layer, into an enormous and abundant experience. This righteous and priceless experience a leader has at his command is very much different from the 'experience' most of today's managers, again mostly in the Public Sector, 'possess'. The leaders possess and demonstrate their altruistic wisdom and winning skills for the complete benefit of the organization in the true sense of the word. They command but do not demand respect. They remain at the forefront and lead from the front when the situation demands, putting their own interests at the rear. They rise to the occasion, irrespective of where they are, what they are, and what situation they are in. They do not look for crowds for following them and do not wait for instructions. They do not succumb to pressure. They draw the lines and set deadlines first for themselves and then for others. These immaculate qualities of a leader are not easy to acquire. Over the years, these traits get consolidated into an invaluable and far-reaching experience. And this experience is something that is gradually acquired *on the ground with a consistent toil*, but not overnight in the cozy comfort of air-conditioned rooms.

With a view to ensuring the acceptable continuity of your credibility, you, therefore, need to consistently introspect yourself in order to know whether you are a 'manager' in the real sense of the word, ready to graduate as a leader, and then on as a mentor, or, a 'damager' with a score of less than 5 on the scale of 1 to 10 against each assenting factor listed above. In order to fit into the former category of managers, leaders, and mentors, you need to become a shining example to your successors in your thoughts, words, and actions. *If one wants to shine like the Sun, then one has to burn like the Sun,* as said by the late Dr. APJ Abdul Kalam. All of us perhaps definitely want to shine like the Sun! Don't we? The question is, how many of us really want to burn like the Sun too? Burning doesn't happen if we do not pass through the fire! How many of us are ready to pass through the fire (testing times)? If we do pass through the testing times, as a consequence, an absolute refinement occurs in us. For this cherished refinement process to start, we need to *undergo consistent toil on the ground,* as just stated. There are absolutely no shortcuts here. Else, as already branded as "Damagers" by the grand old man of Rajasthan, the employees mostly working in the Public Sector, run the risk of being collectively and factually labelled as such.

Let me quickly add here that the factuality of being either a manager or a damager is not limited to one's official position only; it can well be extended to one's personal life too. Whatever your role is, father, mother, son, daughter, brother, sister, friend, neighbour, etc., in each role knowingly or unknowingly you may have been either recognized as an effective manager or already categorized as a damager. Hence, in order to exactly know one's performance level, each and every individual must take this test. We can put everyone in society, on this planet, through this test and gauge his ability to deliver the goods in trying times. When the time is tough and demanding, that is the real-time when we are required to stand the test. If we clear the test with a minimum score of 5 against each of the ten assenting factors and an aggregate score of a minimum of 50, we are clear winners and the real managers, in the right sense of the word.

So, try to bring out the real manager in you irrespective of the position you are in and irrespective of the place you are at, first for the betterment of your own personality, then your family, the environment around you, the organization you are in, and as a consequence, for the betterment of the country you live in, as a whole. For this, you need to first identify for yourself whether you are a manager or a damager, which is the theme underlying this article. The idea is to bring to the fore the damage the people around you and the organization you work for would suffer if you indeed are categorized as a damager.

In the scuffle between these two, which is the title of this article, an organization would clearly lose if its rolls were filled with even a single damager, not to speak of the irreparable damage that is caused to the organization if damagers outstrip its managers. In case the peer evaluation scores categorize you as a damager, and you honestly know it, then you need to urgently take all that is necessary to reverse the damaging situation you are wantonly (maybe unknowingly also) causing and creating, and elevate yourself to the level of a manager and beyond. Once you establish yourself as a real manager, then you can strive further and further to reach the Leader and Mentor levels in your journey towards achieving a meaningful HDI (Human Development Index), the ultimate directory, which clearly specifies your final ranking. You can't afford to lose time any further...the time for this introspection and for taking the litmus test on the scale of 1 to 10 has arrived. And the test must be taken right away.

It's time to take this important decision NOW, and simultaneously act upon it by putting your heart and soul into it! Are You Ready To Do So?

--//--

6

Who Knows You Better Than You?

Which part of our body do we feed first, after bidding farewell to the bed every morning as a new day unfolds in our lives? Is it the part of the body that is neck below, or that part of the body, which is neck up? In well almost nine out of ten cases, the first feed is certainly to the part of the body that is neck below, i.e., the belly; but not definitely to the part of the body that is neck up, i.e., the brain! Do we care to utilize the only two media, viz., our eyes and ears, by effective use of which only we can feed our grey matter, the brain, as the day breaks? Instead, are we utilizing only our oral cavity to supply something hot/cold inside our belly as the night turns into the day?

Majority of us do not start our day by reading some good book or listening to a few inspiring words of an exceptional individual, thus denying some essential early good food to our reservoir of thoughts. The reading of the morning newspaper over a cup of hot, effervescent coffee as the day breaks, perhaps may be an accepted habit to many of us. And we may thus argue that by virtue of this habit, we are feeding our grey matter first, daily. Above habit perhaps may mean that we are feeding our brains as well as our bellies almost together since we are glancing at the newspaper, while sipping the hot coffee!

But the question again is, by reading the morning newspaper what are we feeding our brains with? As we see, a considerable percentage of the content of the daily newspapers is exclusively devoted to current affairs, which take large space of the paper's front few and rear few pages. And we seldom go through the middles of the middle pages (where high-quality thought-provoking content is printed) in the mornings, either due to lack of interest or 'paucity' of time. As the rising Sun keeps on advancing, we are into the daily chores that keep us tied to our bread-winning routine, which continues right up to the late evenings. Thus, we neglect and put behind the essential need to nurture and mould our thinking process when it's most needed, i.e., before we begin our business/work operations.

As we know, our brains are responsible for the places we are in and the positions we are occupying today. Again, our brains will be responsible for the places we would be in, and the positions we occupy tomorrow too! What we are today is the result of the cumulative accumulation of the education, experience, and culture, et al we gained over the years, till yesterday. What we would be tomorrow will be the result of the cumulative accumulation of the education, experience, and culture, et al we gained over the years, till today. i.e., what we gained or did today in terms of any virtue or vice would get added to what we were till yesterday and gets reflected in our situation tomorrow! So, where we would be and what we would do tomorrow is essentially based on what we did today! This is irrefutably true both in the case of a welcome positive development that unfolds in our lives tomorrow or a deplorable negative event that confronts us tomorrow as a result of whether what we did today was either commendable or condemnable, respectively!

Hereinafter, wherever a reference is made to one gender in the text, it equally applies to the other gender too.

What we feed our brains with, decides how we fare. If the feed is wrong and negative, so our behavior, action, and performance are, and vice versa. So, ultimately what we feed our brains with, is much more important than whether we feed our brains or not, which means, rather than putting negatives into our brains, it is altogether better if we do not feed anything at all into our brains! Even the name and fame of the world-famous bodybuilders and wrestlers too are the result of their brains...not of their bodies! For, it is the brain that tells them how to counter and conquer the opponent's moves, in the absence of which their bodies are nothing but a mere bag of muscles, an ensemble of stuffed skin. As Mohammad Ali once said, "I hated every minute of my training. But I told myself, suffer now and live the rest of your life as a champion". The Great Ali knew very well the value and indispensability of training, in the absence of which, he would never have become a champion.

Here, training essentially means the training of the mind first to win or lose. Training of the body comes only next. Unless the mind believes in victory, the body will not even be prepared for it!! It is the mind that prepares the body for victory.

Hence, the old adage "An idle man's brain is a devil's workshop" may require a significant correction. In place of the above, the new adage should be "A man's brain with negative feed is a devil's workshop" since a human being, whether idle or busy, as long as there is no negative feed to his brain, is any day much better than a human being, again whether idle or busy, whose brain is pumped with negatives. As such, we need to decide whether we allow negatives to encroach upon our brains or not. Apparently, it is every individual's responsibility to allow information into his brain only after filtering the negatives. We all know, what destruction and damage a negative mind is inflicting everywhere in today's world...

As we have been observing, in some homes the day starts with brawls and scuffles very adversely affecting not only the environment inside the homes, but the mental outfit of the children present there so much so that, they grow with vices like fear, anger, hatred, et al, resulting in these vices stamping the tiny brains of the innocents with those perilous impressions. Result? The child grows up only to become a nervous individual, unable to accomplish anything worthy in life or turn out to be an anti-social element, delivering deadly blows and causing untold misery first to his family and then to the society at large, causing myriad suffering to all those living around.

Another important aspect to ponder is, how casual and laid-back a human being can become when it comes to extending help to other needy human beings. Humanitarian attitude is something that is the exclusive reserve of humans. Yet, this particular virtue is something that is badly missing in humans today. People who can be coined as excellent human beings (who are venerated and looked up to by all sections of people across the globe) are indeed a rare sight. We are not sure how many decades it may take for this country to produce another great human being like Dr. A.P.J. Abdul Kalam, whom this generation has seen in flesh and blood, or another Mahatma, whom the entire world has recognized as a great soul! Let me cite here the famous quote of Einstein about the Mahatma. "Generations to come will scarce believe that such a one as this in flesh and blood ever walked upon this earth". What Einstein had said about Gandhi might be a revelation to all those of our own country, who in their sheer ignorant blindness, make an eccentric attempt to measure Gandhi as an ordinary mortal and belittle him. Gandhiji was too high a towering personality to even be measured, let alone belittled!

Having been born as humans, why we are miserably failing to live like humans? Why there is an increasing tendency to show off as humans, in the shiny garb of a pseudo halo, while the actual content and intent present in us clearly indicate that we are not? Can't we kill that demon living sometimes covertly and sometimes overtly inside us? Are we doing something sensible to alleviate the pain of our family members or our fellow humans? Or, are we wantonly doing something insensible to elevate their pain and suffering?

No one from the sky up needs to come down to tell us what is proper and what is not. We entered this world with that skill of discretionary judgment meticulously embedded into our body system by our makers. Still, we despondently fail to differentiate between good and bad, propriety and impropriety, grain, and chaff. If we peep deep inside us, we can understand that four factors play a dominant role in bringing that judgmental quality lying inside us to the surface. These are:

1. the environment we live in
2. the way we are brought up
3. the association we keep, and
4. our willingness to get moulded for the better

During the wonderful process of growth from an innocent child to a conscientious and assiduous adult, our aim should be to gradually transform, acquire wings and reach the pinnacle of success in our race to the ultimate peak called HUMANITY! As a child, while the first 2 situations stated above (the environment we lived in, and the way we were brought up) are totally outside our control, but as we grow up and mature into prudent adults, the next two situations (the association we keep, and most importantly, our willingness to get moulded for the better) along with the first situation (the environment we live in) unquestionably lie within our control. These three factors, therefore, are quite decisive in our lives as we grow into adults and determine the direction our lives take thereafter.

The moot question now is, how many of you are really serious about these three factors stated above, and adding value to your lives by choosing the right environment to live in, embracing the right association, and allowing yourselves to get moulded by someone whom you adore as a mentor? Though your present environment is shoddy, and you are in a dreadful association that keeps you away from mentorship, still you do not resist and continue to get swayed away by the temporary comfort your current circumstances are providing, for reasons best known to you. Though you put up an altogether new face when confronted, still when left alone, you continue to do what you do despite knowing that what you are doing is not right. Of course, *who knows you, better than you?*

In the process of your growth, are you first measuring up to the expectations of your makers and then your neighbourhood at large, where you live? Have you ever paused a little and thought? During your official routine, which is different from your personal routine, you need to perform different roles and discharge different responsibilities. Your profession and position predominantly decide the role you are expected to play in society. As a part of the single human race, your role is fixed; to behave and discharge your functions just like a human, a civilized human! But, while discharging your official functions, your roles vastly vary. However differently your roles/functions vary, the one common ingredient that must not be absent as you play your roles is "Humanity".

Unfortunately, especially in today's environment, this common ingredient is getting completely eroded and many humans are behaving worse than beasts, both within and outside their families, which is a disgrace to mankind. You pretty well know whether your behaviour and approach are in line with the decorum of the place where you live and work, or not. You pretty well know whether your reactions to a particular situation are justified from the humanitarian point of view, or not. Internally though you know that the approach you adopted was not the right one, yet you show off the opposite way. You know for sure that there were very big gaps in your life so far. You know for sure that you have not yet accomplished anything significant in your life so far from the humanitarian point of view. You know for sure that what you did to your spouse, sibling, child, another family member, colleague, subordinate, a fellow human, or even to the surrounding fauna and flora was not right. Yet you try hard to argue and defend yourself with all your might that you were right, and you always refuse to accept the truth. Worse, sometimes you feign innocence! Of course, *who knows you, better than you?*

You do several things, good or bad or both, as the day unfolds. You help a few; you dump a few. You love a few; you hate a few. You commend a few; you condemn a few. You promote a few; you demote a few. You reward a few; you punish a few. You make promises; you break promises. You lie to people, yet you don't like when others lie to you. You celebrate your success; you feel jealous of others' success. You tender animals; you tease animals. You raise animals; you kill animals. You protect the environment; you destroy the environment. You eat food, you waste food. You take care of your life; you damn care for others' lives. You fight for a cause; you give up a cause. You take others for granted; yet, you do not want others to take you for granted. You take bribes; yet you complain about others taking bribes. The list is endless...

Have you noticed one thing? It outlines several excellent as well as terrible things you do regularly and *consciously*! What is that single factor that prompts you to do what you do? Is it the dangerous six-letter word HATRED, or the inexcusable five-letter word, GREED, or the most desirable four-letter words, NEED and LOVE? Or, any fifth factor, other than these four? Well, for the vast majority, the two factors that decide why they do what they do are unquestionably HATRED and GREED arising out of a sick or polluted mindset caused due to the feeding of negatives to their brains. For the minuscule minority, the two factors that regulate their actions are NEED and LOVE arising out of a healthy and clean mindset caused due to the feeding of positives to their brains. Most of what you do is out of greed and/or hatred; yet you claim, what you do is out of genuine need and/or love. Of course, *who knows you, better than you?*

There are yet a few people who just do nothing! These people just idle away their time! They, in fact, are also busy doing something--idling away their time! And they have a perfect reason to say in support of their inaction too! They often say they are down with too many problems, that they have lost count of their problems, in view of which they are constrained to stay inactive! Rather than trying to figure out the reasons for their failure to remain active, they conveniently attribute the successful actions of others to a 'problem-less' situation, always complaining about something like 'non-availability of a level playing field' for themselves! This is the exclusive characteristic of the meek and the weak, who are pathetically not aware of the fact that *difficulties in life do not come to destroy them but to help them realize their hidden ability and power. In view of their appalling attitude, they are just ignorant of the fact that willpower and unceasing determination will always triumph in life's worst battles.* They always tend to ignore the fact that a 'level playing field' is something everyone needs to create for himself.

Difficulties, if at all surround you, must know that you are difficult to be defeated. Can you become problematic to the Problems, difficult to the Difficulties, and painful to the Pain so that the so-called Problems, Difficulties, and Pain cannot venture to even look at you, let alone come near you? Even if they happen to lurk in your vicinity, like a black cat in a dark room (where the cat, though definitely present, cannot be seen because the room is dark and the cat is black), they cannot stand the electrifying presence of your towering personality; they have to run away from you to bottomless bottoms and directionless directions, wandering and wandering aimlessly in a spiral, far away from you!!

Ultimately, when someone mentors you and brings you out of your inactive mode, encourages you to take up some worthwhile activity and you succeed at that, and when you were asked to share the secret behind your success, you, despite knowing that someone somewhere at some point of time came to your rescue when you were badly down and provided you with a perfect mentorship and a great support, display a big brave face saying that it was all due to your own ability and power, and that you yourself had built your empire facing the severest odds! Of course, *who knows you better than you?*

A small lapse, a mistake, a crime...there is a big difference between the first and second, the second and third, and again the first and third. While a lapse is a slip that is of temporary nature and purely unintentional, a mistake is an error that may or may not have been caused out of intention, whereas a crime is an act or omission prohibited and punishable by law, something caused out of deliberate intent to inflict damage on someone, a well-defined system, or society.

By making this evaluation, I am trying to state that you need to have the courage to clearly identify your wrong actions and categorize them into lapses, mistakes, or crimes and make quick amends in the event your actions resulted in a burden to the people around you, leaving you as a liability on your family/society. You may not like to categorize the crime committed by you into the category of a 'crime', in spite of the fact that your immediate family in particular, or the society at large had to bear the brunt in view of the consequences that arose because of that crime committed by you.

Though the consequences are apparent and clearly visible, though you are internally aware of the fact that you were indeed directly responsible for the consequences, yet, you altogether deny your role in the outcome of those consequences. Even one hundred family counsellings or several interrogations by the authority may not be successful in making you own up your crime. This is particularly true when the crime was an offshoot of a conversation between you and another individual, who confronted you with facts, after seeing you committing the crime. Further, out of you two, the other one is weak, meek & innocent and you, crafty & potent. You, despite admittedly knowing the truth, would feign innocence, when he charges you with the crime presenting all the indisputable facts from which you can't have any escape. Thus, having been fully aware that you would be caught, you effectively destroy all the evidence and even go to the extent of totally eliminating the other person, in collusion with the authority. Effectively masking your crime thus, you keep roaming as if nothing had happened! Of course, *who knows you better than you?*

Now about the question of your credibility. Credibility is one virtue that cannot be acquired overnight. It is the result of years of truthfulness and trustworthiness practiced by an individual even in tough and demanding situations, even if it amounts to a threat to his own reputation sometimes. Your own experience with different individuals over a period of time tells you whether a particular individual is to be trusted or not. The level of trustworthiness of an individual defines his credibility. Credibility is again nothing but the habit of and being penchant for walking the talk and talking the walk, i.e., saying what is done and doing what is said. Credibility is like a transparent door through which your mind can be read by others. The more transparent the door is, the more credible you become. It is your prime responsibility to ensure that the door remains transparent to the full, without even one speck of dust clinging to it making it opaque at that point, obstructing you from the view of the outside world through that point. Every minute, every second, you must strive to wipe off the dust particles from the surface of the transparent door, keeping it absolutely crystal clean all the time.

The moment dust gathers on the transparent door, first making it misty and then opaque, your credibility too comes to a stake, with the dots of mistrust gradually popping up from everywhere, making you unfit to be labelled as a human being...because, credibility is one of the 4 pillars on which the entire structure of humanity stands, the other three being transparency, honesty, and clarity. Surprisingly, rather than the human kingdom, the animal kingdom is bestowed with these virtues!! Though you fully know that your credibility is at stake, which was the offshoot of your own making, yet, you would not accept it and try to put up a fake face, presenting a pseudo front. Of course, *who knows you better than you?*

Why do people behave the way they behave? As is well known, the behavior of people is decided by what goes into their minds, 24 X 7. Hence, will it be possible for someone else to assess you without knowing your mind? What goes into your mind is known only to you. Hundred percent of the past of you is known only to you. Neither your spouse nor your best pal would know it. Similarly, hundred percent of my past is known only to me. This statement holds good in respect of each and every individual on this planet. You know what type of individual you were, what wrong deeds you did, what lies you told, whether some action you took in the past against someone was really justified and warranted, or it was only the result of your ego, or some infructuous decision taken by you in a fit of anger. You only know all this, and no one else. Of course, *who knows you better than you?*

What grow on their own? Weeds or Crops? Certainly Weeds...Do they not? During the rainy season, when you leave the soil of the farm as it is, what come out of the earth on their own? Weeds... Correct? You would certainly not find saplings of mango, pomegranate, et al, or for that matter any edible vegetable plant coming out of the farm earth on its own. Why? Because good things do not take birth on their own, while bad things sprout out just like that! Let alone sprouting out on their own, crops, even after a great deal of attention by the ever-vigilant farmers in protecting them from the vagaries of nature, still do not survive, resulting in the frustrated farmers committing suicides in large numbers across the country. However, once crops stand against the vagaries of weather and survive the regular onslaught by animals due to the consistent toil and constant vigil by the farmer, the grateful farmer ultimately reaps the harvest to his heart's content with gratitude and feeds the nation to his delight. From sowing the seed to collecting the seed, it is a very big and long-drawn process, involving unimaginable effort.

Now about weeds. Leave them as they are and over a short period of time, they spread a lot taking a good space of the farmland under their cover. Weeds do not require any protection either from the vagaries of weather or from animals. They thrive even in the harshest weather and regrow with double the strength, all the more they are grazed upon. Weeds not only grow on their own, but multiple at a short time, and when found amidst crops, throw the biggest challenge to the poor farmer, who has to put in double the effort first to survive his own crop and second, to kill the weed from killing his crop.

Similarly, negative thoughts, like weeds, encroach upon the land of your tiny brain and take command of it, with the single motive to push you to the destructive path. Unless they are confronted right at the doorstep leading to your brain, their unabated onslaught would continue.

But how to confront the negatives? Simple; by diluting them with positives, i.e., by reading some essentially good stuff and listening to some essentially good stuff and seeing some essentially good stuff on a regular basis. Good thoughts, like crops, are highly sensitive to the environment they exist in. Even if there is a slight change in the environment, the good thoughts would not be able to stand the change and succumb to bad thoughts. Unless you are strong enough to counter the negatives, you would not be able to defeat them. Though your behaviour, your attitude, and your track record, all point out at the rise of negatives within you, you still maintain the stand to the contrary, not willing to be labelled as someone gripped by these drawbacks. You vehemently try hard to project yourself as immune to negatives...Of course, *who knows you better than you?*

For the entire human race to establish that the race indeed consists of humans, it is essential that all of us honestly prove that we, without doubt, are humane (with that human touch), credible, transparent to the core, a reservoir of good thoughts, good words, and good actions, and not greedy. It is essential for us to prove that we are here on this planet to alleviate the pain of our fellow humans but not to paint on the pain of our fellow humans. It is essential for us to prove that the element called "Humanity" is present in us. It's really unfortunate that we, the 'super humans', are required to prove that we are indeed humans! But it's the stark truth! And the effort is definitely not easy; it's very tough, and demanding, and requires real and long-time effort and sacrifices.

You must hence imbibe the real humane qualities so as to ensure that the world also knows you, exactly the same way as you know yourself. You must make all-out efforts to project the real 'you' in you so that no one points his finger *also at you* and say, *who knows you better than you* when the situation to prove your veracity comes. You must make a promise to yourself that you ever remain true to yourself and the world around you, come what may. The time has arrived for remaining honest at least to yourself...

It's time to take this important decision NOW, and simultaneously act upon it by putting your heart and soul into it! Are You Ready To Do So?

--//--

7

Barriers Vs Bridges

What should one aim to become in life? A Medico? A Technocrat? An Attorney? A Bureaucrat? A Barrier? or, A Bridge? Well... the choices available in front of us especially in today's fast-changing world are in fact, innumerable. The choice to choose our profession/occupation undoubtedly rests with each one of us. However, we should exercise enough caution before picking up our choice from the endless list; else, we would rue our choice life-long...since, after a few years into our 'chosen' field, we may not be left with any further choice to switch our choice to another choice!

As the choice to choose our profession/occupation is well within our own hands, it is again absolutely in our own hands whether we want to become a barrier or a bridge within our chosen profession/occupation. So to say, the field we are in at the macroscopic level, and what we look forward to becoming in life at the microscopic level, all shall become relevant and worthy only if we choose to become a bridge rather than a barrier to human *progress, happiness, and development* in our chosen field! And it is also equally true that our lives would become a massive liability and slurred if we again choose to become a bridge rather than a barrier to human *regression, misery, and decay* in our chosen field. Does it then mean, we need to become bridges somewhere and sometimes, and barriers also somewhere and sometimes but not, only either, everywhere and all the time? Let's explore...

The choice to become either a barrier or a bridge must be taken based on the situation we are surrounded by, i.e., this decision must always be situation-specific and hence should never be generalized. Let me offer certain clarity here. We cannot afford to become a bridge always, everywhere, in every situation, and to everyone. Similarly, we cannot afford to become a barrier always, everywhere, in every situation, and to everyone. Before becoming a barrier or a bridge, we, therefore, need to essentially question ourselves on the essentiality factor involved, looking at the genuine interests (but *not* the damaging interests) of the people around us, the organizations we work for, and the nation we represent.

Suppose we want to become bridges... Great! But bridges to what and for whom? Or suppose we want to become barriers... Again great! But barriers to what and for whom? Becoming bridges to issues of national concern and similarly becoming barriers to issues of national interest would be unquestionably catastrophic. What I clearly mean here is, exactly the opposite should be the sole overriding criteria for our decisions in this context. i.e., we must become strong bridges to all the issues and elements of social and national interest and equally strong barriers to all the issues and elements of anti-social and anti-national interest. We must clearly know when to become a bridge and when to become a barrier and we should always be prepared to don both the mantles depending on the situation we are surrounded by, as just stated!

So, while discharging our functions in our chosen fields we need to consciously and consistently check whether we are becoming bridges to development, human happiness, and progress, or barriers to development, human happiness, and progress. However high and might, or low and light we may ultimately become in life, two factors, viz., i). how we influence the people around us for the better by virtue of our position and ii). the decisions we take to become either a bridge or a barrier or both, again for the better, determine our intrinsic value. Before proceeding further, let me first enlighten you with an eye-catching incident from which the title of this article has been coined!

The prelude to the opening question that adored the first line of this article was the amazing scene I saw in the media during the worst floods that hit our own beautiful state of Kerala (God's own country) in the August of 2018. The extraordinary picture was showing a local fisherman, Shri K.P. Jaisal, kneeling on his knees and hands in the knee-deep flood waters, and converting his back into a steppingstone to help the women and children to climb over him to reach the waiting rescue boat. With his studious and reflective kneeling posture on all his four in murky waters, in the middle of what seemed to have once been a road, the water coming up to his shoulder level, Jaisal remained rooted firmly to the ground below as a line of women and children used his back, stamping it with their feet, with their footwear on, to reach to the safety of an inflatable NDRF rescue boat.

What a remarkably humane gesture! How was it possible for this common man to think about such an uncommon service in the first place? A few pics of the humane man extending his service of the highest order to the people in need, in the hour of need, shall help us in understanding the towering personality he is:

Jaisal..The Hero of the masses and the saviour of the Needy...Became a Bridge, literally!!

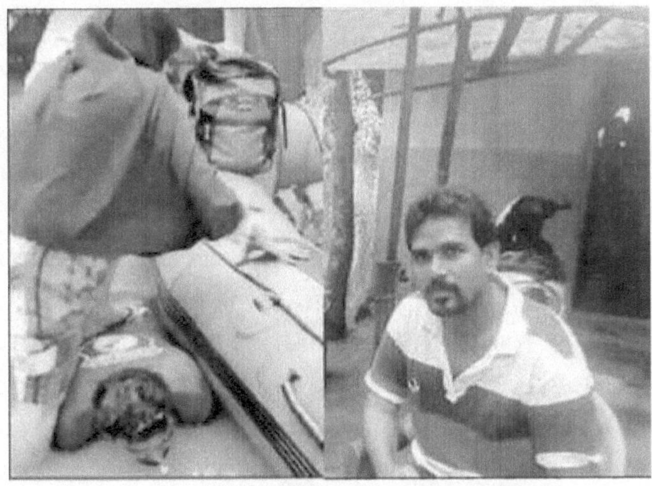

Jaisal was not on hire
But within, full of fire
And he did not tire!
He bore the entire pain
Though nothing was to his gain
And his selfless effort did not go in vain!
He changed his back
Into a Stepping Stone
To help the weak and the meek
Climb onto the boat, risking his own bone!
Putting himself physically Low
He became a Human Bridge!
By doing so, he rose so High
And put to shame the mighty and the rich!!

So, after reading the stupendous and startling story of the "Human Bridge" and the sonnet attempted above in glory of him, what comes to your mind? The adages "The hands that serve are holier than the lips that pray," as aptly professed by Buddha, Mahavira, and Jesus, and "Service to man is service to God," as discoursed by Swami Vivekananda, would have invaded your memory lanes! Right? But again, just memorizing such apt statements is not enough! You need to put them into practice, as our dear Jaisal had shown, by *instantly* rising to the occasion when the situation warranted.

Most of us, if not everywhere and every time, but surely somewhere and at some point in time, must have donned the mantle of either a barrier or a bridge knowingly or unknowingly. If we make an honest attempt to look back into our past, we can feel the visualizations of the damage we had caused to someone at some point in time in one form or the other or, the comfort we had provided to someone at some point in time in one form or the other, due to the roles we played either as barriers or bridges. This means by default, a majority of us are already either barriers or bridges or both, as we are born perhaps with this in-built characteristic. However, the moot question is whether we are playing the said roles for the right reasons or the wrong reasons. If it is for the right reasons, then it's absolutely great! On the other hand, if it is for the wrong reasons, then, it's high time we sat back and made urgent corrections.

The disgusting fact we generally notice is, several people consistently and wantonly become and relish to become barriers or bridges solely for wrong reasons aimed at stalling the progress, happiness, and development of the people around them and for aiding the unscrupulous elements in causing more damage, thus crippling the organizations they are working for and thus of the nation as a whole. Our high positions in life just do not matter, unless our consequent actions are not in line with the needs of the people we live with, the organizations we work for, and the nation we represent.

Why and how do some people instantly become bridges in the true sense of the word for a positive cause like Jaisal, while several others deliberately become barriers to healthy growth and willingly erect stumbling blocks in the path of happiness, progress, and development? What defines the mindsets of these two sets of people? What controls their behavioural pattern? What influences and triggers their action for the better or for the worse? After all, all human beings are alike when they are born! The same innocent looks, the same innocent smiles, and the same innocence all through!

What makes the mental make-up that defines the overall personality of a grown individual that helps him/her don the mantle of a barrier and/or a bridge in the true sense of the word for an absolute and long-lasting positive cause of aiding overall happiness and development?

I have made a small attempt to search for the answers that could address the above concerns. After a considerable search, I have stumbled upon the fact that the answers lie in the presence of humanistic impulse in our thought process, and delighted to note that this great quality amazingly constitutes the single reason that separates man from man!

Recently I have come across a small book titled *"Human Values in Management"* a publication of the extempore lecture series delivered almost 4 decades ago by Swami Ranganathananda, a globally acclaimed scholar-monk of the Ramakrishna Mission & Order, during his address to the officers of the Punjab National Bank (PNB) in New Delhi during Sept 1983. The lectures compiled by PNB were later published by Coal India Ltd, the Maharatna Central Public Sector coal mining behemoth in July 1986, and further later by the Bharatiya Vidya Bhawan under its Eternal Value Booklet Series. What Swamiji had said in the above book was of a lot of relevance then, is now, and shall be in the future too! The book had fortified the search result!

In his address, Swamiji had very strongly and rightly emphasized that education with *human orientation* is the source of all Human Development, and that education of the entire population (not a select population) plays a dominant role in defining the mindset of all human beings for the better and elevates them above the ordinary. Education without selfish motives leads to the enrichment of the students' mental faculties and helps them to clearly see through the haze and realize their avowed responsibilities. This situation ultimately triggers the happiness in and development of themselves first, then of the people around them, and thus ultimately of the overall nation. Here goes what the Swamiji had said 4 decades ago in the book:

"We classify all nations today as developed, underdeveloped, and backward. Our country belongs to the second category. How did the developed nations of today acquire the developed status? They were, some centuries ago, less developed than we are today. In the 15th and 16th centuries, there was much poverty and squalor in Europe. Then came the spread of education among the masses, hard and cooperative work, and human concern. Thus, they became developed, modern science and technology accelerating the process."

In the same context and as quoted from the extracts of Swami Vivekananda's letters included in the same booklet, the following passage on the essential need to spread education to the masses without limiting its fruits to a select few, makes a lot of sense here:

"From the day when education and culture, etc., began to spread gradually from patricians to plebeians (upper classes to the lower classes), grew the distinction between the modern civilization as of Western Countries and the ancient civilization as of India, Egypt, Rome, etc. I see it before my eyes; a nation is advanced in proportion as education and intelligence spread among the masses. The chief cause of India's ruin had been the monopolizing of the whole education and intelligence of the land, by dint of pride and royal authority, among a handful of men. If we are to rise again, we shall have to do it in the same way, ie., by spreading education among the masses...why has originality entirely forsaken the country? Why are our deft-fingered artisans daily becoming extinct, unable to compete with the Europeans? By what power again has the German labourer succeeded in shaking the many-century-grounded firm footing of the English labourer? Education, education, education, alone!"

Drubbing the educated intelligentsia of our country for confining the fruits of education to their own clans and for their own selfish reasons and the serious damage done to the nation as a result of above, Swami Ranganathananda further says in the book:

"Most of our educated people have acquired negative attitudes, along with the dismal fund of self-centredness and callousness; there is a colossal lack of human orientation. There is an urgent need to develop these virtues and graces in all our people, especially this human motivation."

Drawing extensively from Swami Vivekananda, Swami Ranganathananda identifies four factors, the failure to develop which has led to the underdeveloped status of our country. Emphasizing that these four factors are needed to convert our nation back into a fully developed one, he says in the same book:

"Thus, education on a national scale, self-discipline, hard and cooperative work and the humanistic impulse - these are the four means by which under-developed India will become a fully developed nation, with enormous, disciplined energies released from her vast population. We thus free ourselves from our feudal past and become a modern progressive democratic nation, constituting one-seventh of humanity."

A careful perusal of the entire text quoted in the foregoing paragraphs would reveal that people must acquire four factors in order to become responsible citizens with social, rational, and scientific temper, and national bent. These four factors are: first and foremost, *education*, followed by *self-discipline*, then *hard and cooperative work culture*, and finally the *humanistic impulse*, as stated by Swami Ranganathananda. Further, these four factors are instrumental in clearly moulding the mindsets of people and in controlling their behavioural patterns. The judgemental ability thus acquired shall help them to differentiate between the grain and the chaff, the correct and the incorrect, thereby influencing and triggering their actions for the better, and in differentiating a barrier to human happiness and development, from a bridge to human happiness and development. As such these four factors cannot be looked up in isolation and hence must be intertwined so as to deliver the wholesome best results.

In reference to Shri Jaisal, though he may be lacking exposure to formal education, he nevertheless is abundantly blessed with the other three factors, viz., self-discipline, hard and cooperative work culture, and humanistic impulse, with humanistic impulse forming the grand base of the other two. Needless to say, this is the essential characteristic every individual must possess, since this forms the corner stone on which the HDI (Human Development Index) technically stands! In order that we have the best possible HDI, the need of the hour, therefore, is to first develop and then extend such a holistic type of educational system with *human orientation* to the entire population that would help them to decide when and where to become a real barrier and when and where to become a real bridge, so that there will be all-round happiness, progress, and development.

It's time to take this important decision NOW, and simultaneously act upon it by putting your heart and soul into it! Are You Ready To Do So?

--//--

8

Ethical Leadership

When we talk about leaders, whose lives radiated compassion and who had placed ethics and values before everything else for the sake of not only their own countrymen but millions the world over, who would come to our minds first? Let me quote a few distinguished names that unequivocally belong to this CLASS of eminent leadership across the globe...Abraham Lincoln, Mahatma Gandhi, Albert Einstein, Mother Teresa, Nelson Mandela, Martin Luther King Jr, Dr. APJ Abdul Kalam... the list definitely **won't** go on and on. Maybe after a few more names, the list invariably stops. The reason, the world may be having several 'leaders', but only a few Ethical, Inspirational & True Leaders, who can be termed as 'humane', with their DNA got intertwined with the thread of humanity! Let's see in brief, as compiled from the pages of history, why and how these leaders occupied a place of undisputed pride in world history as great leaders during the last couple of centuries. Their greatness was associated primarily with their being, first and foremost, humane, and selfless, resulting in the world recognizing them as great and ethical leaders. Hence, before proceeding further, in the chronological order of the years they were born, let's know what made these lives great. Perhaps it may not be possible to see leaders with similar stature in today's world:

Abraham Lincoln (1809-1865): Lincoln, born in Kentucky, USA, was best known for the preservation of the United States and the Abolition of Slavery in America. Turn the pages of America's political history, and you are sure to find one man who clearly outshines all others. Nicknamed 'Honest Abe' or 'Father

Abraham', Lincoln was, by far, one of the most powerful and greatest Presidents that America has ever witnessed.

Rising from a modest beginning, it was his sheer determination and honest effort that led him to the nation's highest office. An astute politician and a proficient lawyer, he played a vital role in the unification of the states and led from the front for the cause of abolishing slavery in the country, eventually giving people equal rights, irrespective of caste, colour, or creed. He envisioned and actually brought to the forefront a truly democratic government that was led by the concept of 'by the people, of the people, and for the people'. He was a saviour of the Union and an emancipator for the slaves. Though in his life Abraham Lincoln has been felicitated with no awards and honours, as there did not exist any then, as for the presidential ranking polls conducted since 1948, Lincoln has been rated at the very top in the majority of polls. His famous quote, *"do I not destroy my enemies when I make them my friends?"* sums up his outlook towards humanity and crystallizes his personality!

 **Mahatma Gandhi (1869-1948):** The Mahatma, born in the Porbandar State of British India (now Gujarat), fondly called the Father of the Nation, not only led India to independence from British rule but also inspired movements for civil rights and freedom across the world in several other countries. As a lawyer in South Africa, he first employed non-violent civil disobedience in the resident Indian community's struggle for civil rights and was known for his religious tolerance, simplicity, and strong moral values. After his return to India in 1915, he set about organizing peasants, and urban laborers to protest against the imposition of excessive land tax, salt tax, and discrimination. While Independence movements around the world were stained with bloodshed, Gandhi became decidedly famous for fighting for freedom with non-violent means of civil disobedience and non-cooperation. In the months following partition, he undertook several fasts unto death to promote religious harmony. As an enviable

social activist, he fiercely campaigned for women's rights and the reduction of poverty. He was widely known for his philosophy of truth, indomitable courage, and non-violence. His famous quote, *"An eye for an eye will only make the whole world blind"* brilliantly sums up his passion and compassion for the welfare of the people and his ideology of non-violence, which he practiced till his very end. His birthday, 2nd October, is observed worldwide as the International Day of Non-Violence as a fitting tribute to the great soul and in recognition of his steadfast practice and preaching of non-violence and peace throughout his life.

Albert Einstein (1879-1955): Einstein, the German-born physicist, known as the Father of Modern Physics, was honoured with the Nobel Prize in Physics for the law of photoelectric effect in 1921. Do you fondly call the whiz kid in your class/ organization 'Einstein'? If yes, then you aren't the only one who does so. People around the world honour their friends and acquaintances with the title of 'Einstein' for the person's immaculate brilliance and genius mind. While there may be many genius minds set at work to this date, only once in a century an Albert Einstein is born.

The 19th century not just witnessed the birth of Albert Einstein, but with it, the birth of modern physics. Rightly known as the Father of Modern Physics, Albert Einstein was, without a doubt, the most influential physicist of the 20th century. With his research and finding, Einstein created a revolution in the field of science. Amongst his numerous works: (a) the general theory of relativity, which provided a unified description of gravity as a geometric property of space and time, and (b) the photoelectric effect that established the quantum theory within physics are the most important ones. During his lifetime, Einstein published more than 300 scientific papers, apart from 150 non-scientific works. He was the proud recipient of numerous awards. Other than these, he has also been credited by Times magazine as the

Person of the Century. Such was his contribution to mankind that his name has been made synonymous to being "genius". His famous quote, *"I am enough of an artist to draw freely upon my imagination. Imagination is more important than knowledge. Knowledge is limited. Imagination encircles the world"* perfectly emphasizes his belief in the power of creative minds.

 **Mother Teresa (1910-1997):** Clad in a white, blue-bordered sari, Theresa, along with her sisters of the Missionaries of Charity became a symbol of love, care, and compassion for the world. The Blessed Teresa of Calcutta, known the world over as Mother Teresa, was an Albanian-born Indian citizen who abided by her religious faith of Roman Catholicism to serve the unwanted and uncared people of the world. One of the greatest humanitarians of the 20th century, she led all her life serving the poorest of the poor. She was a ray of hope for many, including the aged, the destitute, the unemployed, the diseased, the terminally ill, and those abandoned by their families. Blessed with profound empathy, unwavering commitment, and unshakable faith since young, she turned her back to worldly pleasures and focused on serving mankind ever since she was 18. After years of service as a teacher and mentor, Mother Teresa experienced a call within, which changed her course of life completely. Founder of the Missionaries of Charity, with her fervent commitment and incredible organizational and managerial skills, she developed an international organization that aimed towards helping the impoverished. For her service to humanity, she was honoured with the Nobel Peace Prize in 1979. She was canonized by Pope Francis on 4 September 2016. Her famous quote *"If you judge people, you have no time to love them"* completely sums up her strong conviction in unconditionally serving the hapless people.

Nelson Mandela (1918-2013): Ironically, his baptized forename, 'Rolihlahla' meaning 'trouble-maker', blended well with his personality

over the growing years, as Nelson Mandela, born in a small village in Cape Province, then part of South Africa, caused serious trouble to the government of South Africa, through his anti-apartheid movement and revolutionary ways. Inheriting the 'proud rebelliousness' and 'sense of fairness' from his father, Mandela was raised in a Methodist Christian community.

Since his childhood, he was actively involved in anti-colonial politics, which led to his joining the ANC (African National Congress). The admittance was a historic one not only in the life of Mandela but that of every countryman of South Africa, as it eventually led to a discrimination-free country. Inspired by Gandhi and committed to the non-violent struggle, Mandela however moved to armed struggle after a phase of time. This was basically due to the failure of non-violent protest against apartheid and increasing repression and violence from the state. In his 67-year-long political career, Mandela led numerous movements and was arrested, convicted, and imprisoned various times, the longest being the 27 year-life imprisonment. However, all the pain was worth it as the year 1994 marked the end of apartheid and the holding of multi-racial elections. What's more, Mandela became the inaugural President of the country (apart from being the first black South African to hold the office). Probably, this is why he is referred to by numerous titles, including 'the father of the nation', 'the founding father of democracy', 'the national liberator, the saviour, South Africa's Washington and Lincoln rolled into one'. His famous quote *"when a man is denied the right to live the life he believes in, he has no choice but to become an outlaw"* describes his firm belief in the freedom of people.

Martin Luther King Jr (1929-1968): Born in Atlanta, Georgia, USA, Martin Luther King Junior was a leader of the African-American Civil Rights Movement. While fighting against the injustice meted out to the African-Americans, he carefully shunned violence. His ideas were based on Christian doctrines but for operational techniques he looked towards Mahatma Gandhi's non-violent movement.

His first major campaign was the Montgomery Bus Boycott. It not only led to the abolition of racial segregation on Montgomery's public transport system but also turned King Jr into a national figure and the fiercest spokesperson of the civil rights movement. Subsequently, he led many other nonviolent campaigns and gave many inspiring speeches. Later, he expanded the ambit of his movement and started fighting for equal employment opportunities. His 'March to Washington for Jobs and Freedom' was one such campaign. In his short life, he was arrested twenty-nine times. He dreamt that one day every human being would be judged by his ability, not by the color of his skin. He died from a white fanatic's bullet at the age of thirty-nine. In 1964, Martin Luther King Jr. received the Nobel Peace Prize for his non-violent campaign against racism. He also received the Presidential Medal of Freedom (1977) and Congressional Gold Medal (2004) posthumously. His famous quote *"If I wish to compose, write, or pray or preach well, I must be angry. Then all the blood in my veins is stirred, and my understanding is sharpened"* sums up his fiery and total commitment to the civil rights of the people.

Dr. APJ Abdul Kalam (1931-2015): Our own missile man of India, Dr. A.P.J, born in Rameswaram, Madras (now Chennai), was a prominent scientist who served as the 11th President of India from 2002 to 2007. Renowned for his pivotal role in the nation's civilian space programme and military missile development, he made significant contributions to India's Pokhran-II nuclear tests in 1998 which established him as a national hero. An alumnus of the prestigious Madras Institute of Technology, Kalam began his career as a scientist at the Aeronautical Development Establishment of the Defence Research and Development Organization (DRDO). He was later transferred to the Indian Space Research Organization (ISRO)

where he served as the project director of India's first Satellite Launch Vehicle (SLV-III) programme. He eventually re-joined DRDO and was closely involved in India's defence programme. He served as the Chief Scientific Adviser to the Prime Minister in the 1990s before becoming the President of India in 2002. Immensely popular during his term, he earned the moniker of People's President. Though he was a career scientist, he loved teaching and was truly compassionate at heart. He was honoured with several awards including the Bharat Ratna, India's highest civilian honour, for his contribution to the nation's space and nuclear programme. He considered teaching as the noblest of professions and breathed his last while addressing the students at IIM/ Shillong.

A scientist-philosopher, Dr Kalam came to be known as a protagonist of societal transformation through scientific development and innovation that involved raising the standards of governance and safeguarding the sanctity of public institutions. As a visiting professor to several Universities world-over, Dr Kalam, the scientist-statesman, visited numerous schools, colleges, and Universities across the length and breadth of the country and interacted with over one million schoolchildren and students. Dr. Kalam received honorary doctorates from 40 Universities across the globe and the prestigious King Charles-II Medal from the Royal Society UK, amongst several others, for his contribution to the promotion of science. His famous quotes *"If you want to shine like the sun, first burn like the sun"* and *"Strength respects strength"* grandly sum up his vision for the development of India.

Having read about the 7 greatest leaders the world has ever produced, what do you think is the common quality they possessed, that has kept them in a single line and above the rest? Undeniably, it is their love for humanity and the freedom they longed for humanity! The values they possessed and nurtured! The non-compromising approach and completely selfless nature they practiced when it came to observing life's principles! Their attitude to always GIVE and their Ethics!

I would explicitly say that humanity is the single quality that should be considered ultimate and must be looked into when we differentiate leaders from leaders. Again, when I use the term 'humanity, I consciously say that the word covers the entire environment on earth, the fauna and flora included, but not just that, which is specific to humans. Thus, any leadership which does not care for humanity, simply cannot be called leadership, let alone called "Ethical Leadership".

Practicing Leadership is entirely different from practicing Ethical Leadership. When we simply talk about 'leaders', there are several of them; in fact, in the present-day scenario, a 'leader' is getting popped up, created, or installed, at the drop of a hat; and again, these leaders are either self-styled or projected. Worse, a few 'leaders' force themselves on the people, robbing them of their freedom and taking them for granted against their will. Needless to say, these 'leaders' are in fact not leaders, but blighters and are thus a big liability on society. What the world or for that matter, a nation, needs are not the 'self-styled', 'projected', or 'forced' leaders, but those on whom the mantle of leadership falls on its own and whom the nation consciously chooses by virtue of their great and ethical qualities. Let's examine what these qualities are:

First and foremost, a leader must be humane, as already said in the beginning, to be called ethical; by being humane, I mean he/she must possess a very high degree of compassion for other fellow human beings, the fauna, and the flora, i.e., the whole environment in which he/she lives. A humane leader puts his own life at peril when the situation demands and goes to any extent to protect the lives of the people around him. A humane leader is a complete leader.

The second quality I look for in an ethical leader is, he/she must be humble. As a fruit-bearing tree always bends down, a leader who bears virtues always remains humble by the weight of his/her virtues. The unique thing about having virtues is, while the weight of virtues makes the leader stay on the ground, the presence of the very virtues makes the leader's aura fly high! A leader with virtues takes the blame himself/herself for failure, and passes on credit to others for success. A virtuous leader is a lustrous leader.

The third quality is nobility. Being noble, or being righteous, is very difficult and this is a virtue that cannot be acquired easily. One has to toil hard and face innumerable testing times to prove one's nobility or righteousness. A person's righteousness comes to the fore when he/she operates under a conflict of interests. When the interests of his/her own blood relations are at stake and the person puts righteousness before everything else and impartially decides in favour of the affected, that is when his/her nobility surfaces. A noble leader is a global leader.

The great ethical Leader par excellence this generation has seen in flesh and blood was, undoubtedly, Dr. APJ Abdul Kalam. It may be appropriate here to quote what Dr. APJ had said about the 'specific quality' of 'leaders' we see today and how they somehow continue with their so-called leadership with the support of followers and how the concept of 'to lead' has become their greed.

In one of his best sellers, *"You Are Born to Blossom"*, Dr Kalam says: *"The second most important desire after immortality is 'to lead.' Man is bestowed with the trait to preside over other creatures on the earth. This trait overdeveloped into a desire to lead fellow beings and govern their affairs. One can govern oneself, or one can govern the whole earth. In between, we may find leaders who operate primarily within families, communities, states, and nations. Intertwined with such categories, and overlapping them, we find religious leaders, workplace leaders such as executives, officers, managers, team leaders, supervisors, and leaders of voluntary associations. Though there are many stories to make us believe that charisma and personality worked miracles, most leaders operate within a structure of supporters and executive agents who carry out and monitor the expressed or filtered-down will of the leader. This undercutting of the importance of leadership may serve as a reminder of the existence of the follower."*

In another of his famous book, *"A Manifesto for Change – A Sequel to India 2020,"* Dr. Kalam defines the qualities of a true leader, an ethical leader, as below:

1. *A leader must have a vision*

2. *A leader must have a passion to realize the vision*

3. *A leader must be able to travel the unexplored path*

4. *A leader must know how to manage success and most importantly, failure*

5. *A leader must have the courage to take tough decisions*

6. *A leader should have nobility in management*

7. *A leader should be transparent in every action*

8. *A leader must defeat the problem and*

9. *A leader must work with integrity and succeed with integrity.*

Thus, ethical leadership is all about harbouring and practicing the above 9 qualities, as espoused by the Missile Man of India along-with being humane and humble, as shown to the world by all the 7 great leaders illustrated, including Dr. APJ himself. You need to make an introspection, so as to ascertain whether you are blessed with the above qualities, or not and whether you can claim that your 'leadership' is acceptable. Here leadership by default refers to 'ethical leadership' at the organizational, State, or National level, or for that matter, any level per se. If the answer to the introspection is in the affirmative, you can continue to be enshrined in your respective leadership role/position. If not, you simply lose your claim. You need to face the ire of the people in the event your claim to ethical leadership proves hollow. For securing a clear answer, you need to take the litmus test, putting your 'ethical' leadership claim to the test of fire! In order to face the test of fire, you require a lot of courage since the test involves subjecting yourself to the public scrutiny of the highest order, the span of the public running across the length and breadth of an organization, province, state, or nation, but not confined to your own limited stronghold. You can't lose time any further for taking the test.

It's time to take this important decision NOW, and simultaneously act upon it by putting your heart and soul into it! Are You Ready To Do So?

--//--

9

Mind Pollution Vs Body Pollution

Between the mind and the body, which is dependent on which? Which controls which? Are they interdependent? Or do they mutually control each other? Or, still better, do they mutually complement each other? Or is it only the mind that controls the body, and the body, in turn, follows each and every instruction of the mind?

The adage *when the going gets tough, the tough get going* amply demonstrates that the toughness of a person is clearly the toughness of his/her mind and when the situation becomes tough for the body, it's the toughness of the mind that takes control and 'dictates' the body to move on!

So, all said and done, can we say that it is only the mind that controls the body, and it is only the body that follows each and every instruction of the mind? If the answer to this straight question is an authentic 'yes', then this well means that the positive the mind's instructions are, the positive the body's actions would be and vice versa. That is, while a *positive or clean mind* delivers constructive instructions, a *negative or polluted mind* delivers destructive instructions, and the body carries out both unhesitatingly with equal seriousness. From this observation, it can be concluded that while the mind is the master, the body is the slave. As we all know, whatever the master says, the slave ought to obey without a question. He always waits for his master's instructions (whether constructive or destructive) and is ever ready (or afraid?) to listen to his master's voice and carry out his instructions. Similarly, the body always waits for the mind's instructions, whether constructive or destructive and follows the said instructions meticulously with all obedience and again, without raising a question!

Hereinafter in the text wherever a reference is made to one gender, it equally applies to the other gender too.

It is yet again only for the mind to either further revise or altogether reverse its earlier instructions too, and the body accordingly changes its course of action 'n' number of times, in line with the mind's changing instructions! Further, while a *clean* mind doesn't contemplate anything ill of others, on the other hand, a *polluted* mind always does exactly the opposite, and the body accordingly acts! Highlighting of a few common actions carried out by the body consequent to the instructions received from a polluted mind may be apt here. These are:

1. rude behaviour

2. yelling, shouting, and brawling inside & outside the homes, workplaces, and public places

3. bulldozing one's way everywhere with scant regard for others

4. finding fault with every action of others

5. denying women, children, sick, infirm, and the elderly their due, not allowing them to board the public transport first, and not offering them seats inside the coaches

6. causing inconvenience in whatever way, to people around

7. use of all places for putting the garbage, other than the garbage bins

8. spitting and/or smoking at workplaces, public places, and on roads

9. non-compliance with civic rules/regulations, traffic rules, etc., e.g., jumping the red signal, and

10. making a mockery of everyone and everything, etc.

All these and several other invasive and offensive actions caused on a daily basis by polluted minds, though simple and normal they may look, do offend the persons at the receiving ends to no end. While this is what we see regularly around us, the massive damage a polluted mind inflicts on & causes to whole cities & nations at times, need not be emphasized.

If the mind intentionally rests, that is the only time when the body also rests! However, when the body rests after a day's severe physical exertion again at the instance of the mind, the body has to instantly wake up in the event the mind jerks it up midway! If the mind retards or becomes defunct, either due to any severe physical injury to, or failure of any vital in-built systems of the brain, the body's movements also consequently become retarded or defunct. Thus, when the mind becomes *'empty'* due to any reason whatsoever, the body doesn't perform, and if at all it performs, such performance is limited only to a few basic innocuous and loose movements.

This being the mind-body relationship, if I hence say that an individual with an *empty mind* is undoubtedly much better than and more preferable to an individual with a *polluted mind,* how many of you would agree? I am sure everyone would, that too without raising a question, since, as we all know, 'no action' is always preferable to a 'damaging action'!

The body follows the instructions of the mind not only without the slightest resistance as already stated, but also without even wanting to know whether those instructions were for the good of society, bad for society, or for that matter, even for the good of itself or bad for itself! Had the body got the ability to analyse the mind's instructions, and applies its own judgment as to the propriety and reasonableness of those instructions before carrying out the same, then all the terrorist acts, anti-social acts, atrocities on women and children, et al and so to say, all illegal acts per se, including suicides and suicide killings, all of which are only carried out by the body (at the mind's instructions), would not have been happening!

But unfortunately, the body is not bestowed with this strategic ability. Thus, when the mind is happy, healthy, and unpolluted, the instructions that are passed on to the body by the mind also stay happy, healthy, and unpolluted, allowing the body to accomplish the tasks assigned to it in a happy, healthy, and unpolluted way, ultimately leading to the creation of a happy, healthy, and unpolluted environment. On the other hand, when the mind is jealous, sick, and polluted, all the consequent actions performed by the body too shall accordingly remain likewise.

Mind pollution thus has very far-reaching consequences with its indisputably destructive capability to tear apart an individual, the family, society, and the country, irrespective of their alliance with or allegiance to the mighty. Whatever the mind wants to do, that has got to be done. This has been amply endorsed by Dr. A.P.J. Abdul Kalam, when he said: *"An ignited mind is the most powerful resource on the earth, above the earth and below the earth."* And Dr. Kalam had further said, *"No sanction can stand against ignited minds."* By saying so, Dr. Kalam meant that the ignited mind, being the power horse, is unstoppable. However, when he used the word 'ignited', what the great APJ had invariably meant was about the positively charged mind contributing to nation-building activities, but not about the negatively charged mind contemplating and executing nation-breaking activities. For the sake of this article, however, I would like to draw the liberty of using the term 'ignited' in both contexts, as the body is destined to discharge every instruction (whether constructive or destructive) passed on to it, by the 'ignited' mind. However, the point to ponder is, the 'ignition' of the mind is for accomplishing what?

Today we all are witness to the irreparable damage being inflicted on thousands of innocents, the weak and the meek, by a few negatively ignited and polluted minds. Every area (whether it is the home, the workplace or a public place) is infected with polluted minds, seriously affecting the harmonious atmosphere prevalent there, by spewing venom into the fresh minds of the people through their polluted tongues that is resulting in wanton and large-scale damage to the safety and security of the people, leaving several wounded, dead and homeless, forcing innocent children to become destitute and causing huge destruction to the possessions and assets belonging to the people and the State. A microscopic section of the people, because of their mind pollution, are responsible for this dreaded and terrific misery inflicted on the larger population. When the polluted mind strikes, desolation starts, and inexplicable destruction is unleashed on mankind. Is this the attribute of a 'civilized' society we are boasting of?

Contrary to mind pollution, I intend to discuss one more pollution from the context of this article, and that is body pollution.

As against mind pollution which normally affects major chunks of the population and becomes a huge barrier to growth abetting mass destruction, body pollution is purely individual-specific. The two common forms of body pollution are those caused to the body either due to the unavoidable exposure to the outside environment in view of one's nature of work/activity, or due to any disease, whether due to wrong lifestyle or otherwise, or any accidental injury to the body. While the first form of body pollution can simply be washed away, the second form can be cured, thanks to the present-day advancements in modern medicine and revival of the traditional medicine. In view of its individual-specific nature, body pollution does not affect society at large. Though mind pollution does not have any role in the occurrence of these two forms of body pollution, however, let me quickly add here that, body pollution sometimes caused to an individual by an accidental injury, or due to something like the recent pandemic that took the whole world under its grip may also be due to the direct or indirect act of a polluted mind.

The third form of body pollution and the resultant injury caused to a hapless woman or a girl child due to sexual abuse/exploitation is the most exasperating, severe, and reprehensible in nature, and this is unquestionably the direct effect of a severely polluted mind. Hence, this category of pollution though per se caused to the body, is essentially grouped under mind pollution. How quickly the affected can overcome the trauma and restores herself to normalcy, depends first and foremost on how quickly the law enforcement agencies bring the guilty to book and mete out an equally traumatic corporal punishment to the perpetrators and executors of the heinous crime, and then, on the mental strength of the affected and finally on the support the affected receives from the family and society.

Though the perpetrators and those who harbour mind pollution being merely a small percentage of the human population, the polluted mind nevertheless, is wreaking havoc not only on the majority of humans but on mother nature also. Beautiful & fertile landforms and big & small water bodies being no exception, the polluted mind is gripping the animal and plant kingdoms also in its treacherous clutches (as by poaching/smuggling), seriously threatening the very existence of the endangered animal/plant species across the globe. Apart from the mind and body pollution, we (animals and plants included) are irrevocably surrounded always by some sort of pollution viz., water pollution, land pollution, noise pollution, air pollution, etc., the source of all of which again is the polluted mind!

Though natural causes like volcanic eruptions and natural forest fires, etc., also lead to a few or all of the above forms of pollution, still mankind need not be concerned about such harsh acts of nature, since nature with its beautiful in-built mechanism of enormous checks and balances, is bestowed with the great ability to counter the ill-effects caused by its own action, undoing the same at quick intervals and restoring its harmonious balance, when left to itself! However, the biggest misfortune is, the present-day man, hell-bent to damage this whole planet, because of his polluted mind, is even interfering in nature's own work and not allowing nature to repair itself and is thus fast digging his own grave because of his arrogance first and due to his ignorance, next.

Thus, all forms of pollution, barring the first two forms of body pollution-with the rider explained, are the direct result of a polluted mind. Therefore, we may finally condense all forms of pollution into only two types, viz., 1). Mind Pollution and 2). Body Pollution. Now the point is, out of these imminent two, which pollution is more tolerable and has fewer consequences? As we have just discussed, obviously it is body pollution, since, in whatever form it occurs, it affects only the individual concerned, contrary to mind pollution, which frightfully has the extreme ability to wipe out not only the entire human race but the entire life forms from this planet, if left unchecked.

Again, between Mind Pollution and Body Pollution, the latter, being external, cannot be avoided. It happens on a daily basis whether we are inside or outside our homes and regular bath, cleansing, washing, and maintenance of personal hygiene and hygiene of the surroundings are the only physical actions needed to keep the body pollution away. On the other hand, mind pollution, being internal, can fortunately be totally avoided. When each and every one of us is highly concerned about our body pollution and taking regular care to keep the agents that cause our body pollution away, why we are not equally concerned about our mind pollution and why can't we exercise similar care to keep the agents that cause our mind pollution also away?

While getting rid of body pollution involves a small amount of physical activity as explained above, getting rid of mind pollution doesn't require any such physical action either! Further, the elimination of mind pollution invariably results in the simultaneous and effective elimination of all forms of the crime rate too, thus contributing to the birth of a crime-free society, which is the basis for the creation of a happy, healthy, and unpolluted environment. When society becomes crime-free, we don't require the police system and even the judiciary, since the society shall be free from criminals and people need not fight long legal battles as there would be camaraderie everywhere and complaints about "crime" and "injustice" would no longer be heard from any quarters and these two dreaded words would soon be forgotten! Is such a situation indicative of the prevalence of camaraderie and amity amongst people, and an adequate proof that all the citizens of such a society do not harbour polluted minds? Will it be possible to have such a utopian society?

Now the first set of important questions: Why the mind becomes polluted in the first place and how one can get rid of this rot? What is the crux of this seriously damaging state of mind?

If we fathom our hearts with a deep insight invoking our inner voices, perhaps it is not impossible to find out the answers. Is it because of the wrong upbringing? Is it because of a wrong association? Is it because of the prevalence of the wrong environment? Or is it because of the serious disparity noticed between man and man? Or is it because of a situation where man is intolerant of his fellow man because of the other man's better position and prosperity in society? Or is it because of the growing tendency to earn easy & quick money? Or is it because the man wants an instant cozy lifestyle without undergoing the pain of gradual and natural processes of wealth creation? *OR IS IT SIMPLY BECAUSE OF THE COMPLETE ABSENCE OF ETHICS AND VALUES?*

A child is never born with a polluted mind and children, when left to themselves, always pitch in for other children. However, as they grow up they become "mature," "learned" and "knowledgeable" under the impact of the "guidance," "influence" and "teachings" they received from parents and society. And over a period, they become "responsible" adults, acquiring adequate "abilities" to "face" their lives. The fact that the keywords in the above sentences are placed within inverted commas is indicative of the hint that all the said words have negative connotations in the context of the above situations, which point out that in quite a few (or several?) households, by the time an innocent child bubbling with enthusiasm and a clean mindset becomes an adolescent, his original persona is already under clout and his mind might well be on its way to becoming polluted.

Result? He starts lying first to his own parents and other kith and kin in the family, next resorts to cheating in examinations, and then in all other matters, acquires other vices and as he turns into an adult, becomes highly self-centered and brays for the blood of his fellow human being. The decay spirals over the years and with each passing day his mind pollution acquires higher dimensions. The single reason behind all this serious scourge is the complete loss of ethics and values in him as he grows, courtesy the "teachings" he received right from an early age from various quarters and the non-availability of a "screen" or "guard" that filters the negatives from the "teachings" from reaching his mind! Can we install these "Mind Screens" or "Mind Guards" on the entire humanity and stall the rot from reaching the minds of people?

And, now the second set of important questions: Is it possible to have an unpolluted mind? and thus, have unpolluted instructions passed on to the body? And thus have an unpolluted and happy situation at home, on the streets, in society, in the nation, and in the world? Though the single answer to the above series of questions based on the general perception (taking into consideration the events currently unfolding around us and in parts of the country and the world) may be a hesitant "NO", still a mountain of certainty to dispel the fears appears on the horizon, lighting up the great hope about complete decimation of the polluted mind, if not sooner, definitely later. However, we need to attach a definite date for achieving this, so that our dream of complete decimation of the polluted mind first from our homes, then from society, then from the nation, and finally from the face of the earth, can become a goal! Otherwise, our dream shall merely remain wishful thinking...

Having thus garnered the mountain of certainty, an attempt is made here to find out the final answer. It is simple. The solution invariably revolves around imbibing ethics and values. Model your own life on these virtues and let your child grow seeing you thus. Build ethics and values into the psyche of your child right from an *early age*. Never compromise on these grand qualities, come what may. Be the Go-Giver!

If the core values are not imbibed right from early childhood, and if you do not continuously instil the fresh minds of your tiny tots and the minds of the younger generation with these values, the entire human race is sure to get annihilated from this wonderful planet, since mind pollution, any day, and any time, is the worst thing to happen. For this NOT to happen, you need to change your attitude for the better. Since practice precedes preaching as propounded by the Mahatma, you need to first develop the habit of harbouring an unpolluted and clean mind yourself, and then only your children shall replicate you.

And the good news is, Mind Pollution can *always* be avoided and ultimately conquered, unlike Body Pollution, which is unavoidable and thus has got to be encountered & cleansed on a daily basis, as already stated.

You cannot afford this dreaded and sea-deep situation of mind pollution prevail inside and around you anymore. Polluted Minds must be replaced with Clean Minds. As the old adage *"Charity Begins at Home"* goes, your home must become the point of origin for this new habit to develop. Be your child's first mentor first, based on these grand qualities!! Slowly, your mentorship finds acceptance in the neighbourhood, in different institutions, and at the State and National levels. Over a period of time, the world shall also gladly accept you as its mentor and embrace your mentorship!!! *AND WHERE MENTORSHIP ON ETHICS AND VALUES EXISTS, MIND POLLUTION EXITS!*

Very concerted efforts by each one of you as outlined in the foregoing paragraphs towards conquering mind pollution are absolutely needed.

It's time to take this important decision NOW, and simultaneously act upon it by putting your heart and soul into it! Are You Ready To Do So?

--//--

10

Intelligence Vs Wisdom

The Oxford Advanced Learner's Dictionary describes *intelligence* as the ability to learn, understand and think in a *logical* way about things, while explaining *wisdom* as the ability to make sensible decisions and give good advice based on the *experience* and knowledge that one has.

The Webster's dictionary defines *intelligence* as the ability to learn or understand or to deal with new or trying situations based on *reason*, which is a rational ground or motive, while explaining *wisdom* as the ability to discern inner qualities and relationships based on *insight*, which is the power or act of seeing into a situation.

The essential features that differentiate *intelligence* from *wisdom* thus being known from two authoritative sources of the English language, it may have become clear that a distinct line demarcates these two vital traits.

Although this important line separating these two traits per se is undeniably distinct, the trick however is, the line appears too thin sometimes, and visibly thick yet other times. While the thick line can be easily noticed enabling us to differentiate between intelligence and wisdom with ease, we need to be intensely focused when the line appears thin; otherwise we may fumble leading to mistaking intelligence to wisdom. Further, intelligence always tries to conceal wisdom under its seemingly innocuous mask!

Hereinafter in the text wherever any reference is made to one gender, it equally applies to the other gender too.

Before proceeding further, a few questions need to be raised and answered, especially in view of the fact that we are witnessing rapid changes all around us in the present-day Information/Digital Age, which is chiefly the domain of the intelligentsia.

Here go the questions and their respective answers:

Sl. No.	Question	Answer
1	Are we somewhere seriously floundering in giving excessive weightage to the so-called 'intelligence component' of an individual, known in today's terms as "Intelligence Quotient" or "IQ"?	*Obviously Yes*
2	Is it only the IQ that determines the overall value of an Individual?	*Definitely No*
3	Can an individual's value be assessed in the absence of IQ?	*Definitely Yes*
4	In the remote event if we indeed believe that IQ does play a role in deciding the overall value of an individual, then what percentage of IQ is needed in an individual so that he can be called a "real" human being?	*Not More than a Zero*

Surprised at the answers? While a section of the individuals may be intellectuals and thus claim themselves to be comprising the so-called think-tank, and thus brand themselves as the privileged class, the hard fact however is, all such intellectuals definitely cannot be counted as real human beings.

Well, if the above statement is true, then what is the first and foremost parameter that gives a "real" human being a distinct identity? What are the other essential qualities an individual must possess so that he can continue to be rated as a real human being? I believe the first and foremost parameter is the sole humanitarian criteria called *compassion*. Whatever high IQ levels an individual may possess, as long as he does not hold and exhibit the unequivocal quality of compassion, he cannot label himself as a real human being.

Now let's discuss the other qualities needed in this regard. Next in line is the willingness to *understand* his fellow human beings and all the fauna surrounding him. The third is the readiness to unconditionally *alleviate* their pain, and the fourth is, the inclination to treat the surrounding nature with *responsibility*. By putting all these four statements together, we may thus define a real human being as *"an individual who readily & unconditionally understands and alleviates the pain of his fellow humans and the nearby fauna with compassion and treats his surrounding nature with responsibility."* Furthermore, all such individuals by default become *acceptable* everywhere and to everyone. In the subsequent pages an attempt has been made to shed more light on the connotations surrounding the *acceptability factor*.

A human being with an innate quality of compassion is thus a real human being, who does not require any IQ, for IQ has no or little role to play in ensuring that humans remain humane! Compassion forming the very roots of the tree of great human qualities, the other three qualities, viz., sense of understanding, unconditional readiness to alleviate of the pain of others, and sense of responsibility are like branches to the tree, and hence by default, these three qualities will be present in all those individuals who are compassionate in the first place. Thankfully, compassion can be acquired even by all those, who are not born with it, but are willing!

In our day-to-day lives, we quite often observe that a *section* of the educated intelligentsia simply doesn't care for their fellow human beings, let alone the surrounding fauna and flora. One significant 'credential' of these people is their superlative ability to trick other people to worry and distress with their extremely manipulative and calculated approach, in the process causing untold misery to their fellow beings. They draw immeasurable pleasure in repeatedly tricking other people to dejection, taking undue advantage of their ignorance, helplessness, or the situation they are in. They muster all their energies to somehow and anyhow put their fellow human beings to discomfort at every available opportunity.

Worse, if any opportunity is not forthcoming by itself, they put all their intelligence to tremendous use and create several such opportunities at superlative speed. Each and every act of them is performed with meticulous planning, which when gauzed even under the most powerful microscope, shall be found to contain not a trace of compassion and other associated humanistic elements. Whatever they think, say, or do, pathetically lack this dash of silver lining. In the process, not only their fellow human beings but the nearby fauna and flora also suffer silent pain and become victims at their hands. Sometimes, in order to satisfy their own conceited pleasures, while they do pay great heed to their immediate fauna and flora, e.g., their pets and plants in their own houses, farms, etc., yet they remain very insensitive to their fellow humans.

Adopting the humanistic approach in whatever we think, say, or do therefore becomes an element of paramount importance in deciding our overall value, and it is precisely in this context that I wish to once again make a reference here to the small yet phenomenal book titled *The Human Values in Management*, which was the compilation of the series of lectures delivered to the officers of the Punjab National Bank (PNB) in New Delhi during September 1983 by Swami Ranganathananda who was a globally renowned and widely respected scholar-monk of the Ramakrishna Order, thinker and an eloquent speaker on the spiritual and cultural aspects of life (earlier reference made to the above book was in the article 'Barriers vs Bridges').

The Swamiji's above impromptu and electrifying talks were subsequently brought into a book form by Punjab National Bank. Three years later Coal India Ltd, the coal behemoth and a Maharatna Central PSU, with kind permission from the Swamiji, published the lecture series in 1986. Further, three years later in 1989, Bhartiya Vidya Bhavan brought out its first edition of the Swamiji's outstanding talk, which was followed by its second and third editions in 1996 and 2006 under Bhavan's Eternal Value Booklet Series.

The point that the hardly 75-page booklet is undergoing reprints for the last almost 4 decades is evidence to the twin facts that i). the contents of the book are eternal and ii). demand rises by default when the product commands respect. And a product commands respect when it comes with quality. Because of its immense qualitative content, the book was relevant then, is relevant today, and shall remain relevant in future as well.

Swami Ranganathananda's imposing talk was greatly influenced by Swami Vivekananda's powerful nation-building and man-making ideas and ideals. Heavily emphasizing on the great need to infuse *human values* into our national life by which we can overcome our accumulated problems challenging our national aim of total human development, and lamenting that science and technology (the exclusive domain of the intelligentsia) had failed to achieve their intended goal in our country after we became independent, Swami Ranganathananda says:

Quote:

"It is obvious that something went wrong with us immediately after we became free, after we rescued ourselves from our long political subjection. Our nation is not lacking in many of the ingredients that go to make for steady national development under the spur of freedom; our people are endowed with intelligence, varied talents, and ambition. Today we boast of being third among the nations of the world in scientific and technological manpower. But what has it meant to the nation at large? What has been its impact on the condition of millions and millions of people? What is wrong with our nation that, with all our talents, and holding the status of being third in scientific and technological manpower resources, more than half of our population is yet sunk in poverty, ignorance, squalor, and suffering? Why have science and technology not achieved in our country the miracles achieved in the developed countries? Why did the blessings of science not

flow from the scientist and his laboratory to the mass of the people in a big way?

The purpose of science, as expounded by Thomas Huxley, the collaborator of Charles Darwin in the 19th Century, was not only the advancement of knowledge but also the 'alleviation of the human suffering'. If the first is to lead to the second, there is a need to wed the pursuit of knowledge, ie., education, with the humanistic impulse. Unfortunately, after independence, we divorced our education, politics, and administration from this humanistic impulse."

Unquote:

Deeply deploring that the country's upper classes and the educated intelligentsia had badly let the country down before and after our independence respectively, Swami Ranganathananda further adds:

Quote:

"Anyone who has studied his (Vivekananda's) literature will be impressed by its constant stress on this human orientation. He awakened our long-dormant national energies and impressed them with this humanistic touch. During our immediate feudal past, there was very little of this human orientation; it was often anti-human, with caste-exclusiveness, untouchability, and human exploitation as its outstanding characteristics. Our upper classes missed the great opportunity then to educate and raise our common people and build up a great nation; not only did they fail to do this, but they also sat heavily on the common people and fattened themselves, by doing which they brought themselves and the common people under the shame of foreign domination and humiliation for centuries.

In spite of this unhappy experience of the immediate past, how did our educated classes slide quickly from the ecstasy of freedom of our Independence Day on 15 Aug 1947 to rank selfishness, human unconcern, and complacency thereafter? Many of our educated countrymen today are 'dead' people because they live for themselves and have forgotten to live for others, forgotten to live and work for the nation. Having got educated at the cost of the nation – for the fees a student pays for his or her education is only a fraction of his or her total educational expenses – he or she has forgotten the nation, neglected to serve it, and raise the rest of the people, they have become traitors to the nation."

For the sake of understanding the sheer ferocity and the tremendous impact of the words of Swami Vivekananda that shook the nation from its deep slumber, it may be apt to reproduce the same below, which constitute the central idea of Swami Ranganathananda's above lecture:

"So long as the millions live in hunger and ignorance, I hold every man a traitor who, having been educated at their expense, pays not the least heed to them. Life is short, the vanities of the world are transient, but they alone live who live for others, the rest are more dead than alive."

Unquote:

Careful understanding of what Swami Vivekananda had said in the above lines would reveal two hard facts: i), we live only when we live for others; ii). we cease to be called traitors to the nation only when we selflessly serve the common people with our knowledge and talents.

Following three important path-breaking revelations would emerge from a perusal of the excerpts from Swami Ranganathananda's lecture quoted in the foregoing paragraphs:

1. The Human Development Index is the single criterion that exclusively reflects a nation's real development

2. Any service pretended to have been 'done' to people without the humanistic impulse is in fact a disservice to the people, and

3. Science and technology are of no use if the benefits derived from them fail to alleviate the misery of the common man

The above revelations would further unfold the fact that the focus of the nation was, is, and shall remain purely and only on those, who are bequeathed with the humanistic impulse (compassion), in whatever they think, speak, or do. People with very little or even zero intelligence levels but **bestowed** with this outstanding quality are the ones the nation is looking for, whereas people with very high intelligence levels but *sans* this quality are unwelcome and a clear liability, as unequivocally pronounced by Swami Vivekananda, and emphasized by Swami Ranganathananda in his awesome talk.

Coming back to the 'acceptability' factor of people, which is in direct proportion to the humanistic impulse (compassion) present in them, I would like to coin the term "Acceptability Quotient" or AQ, in contrast to IQ, in order to measure the acceptability levels of people. While IQ is related to the aptitude of an individual, AQ is purely related to the attitude of an individual. In view of this refreshing difference, AQ is much easier to acquire and improve upon, just like EQ, the Emotional Quotient. And a person with a high AQ level is far more successful and contributing more to his home, society, nation, and the world, rather than a person bestowed with only a high IQ level! Thus, being far more superior to IQ, AQ is the parameter that distinctly stays ahead in bringing people together.

Needless to say, people simultaneously ingrained with equally high IQ & AQ levels together, are nevertheless the prized possessions of any nation and nations need to be blessed with such people in order to become developed nations!! This hard fact may well explain why India is still not counted as a developed nation, even after nearly 7 1/2 decades of political independence. The irony is, while pre-independent India was studded with countless such jewels, post-independent India is terribly lacking such people, as bitterly stated by Swami Ranganathananda in his above lecture.

A brief discussion on the AQ may be relevant here. As individuals, we feel important when we are accepted by everyone and everywhere. Unfortunately, in today's families, corporates, educational institutions, establishments, government, and in public life per se, we often notice that the 'acceptability' factor of people at large is always at stake. It is distressing to note that one member is not acceptable to another in the same family, one employee is not acceptable to another in the same office, and one political leader is not acceptable to another in the same political party. Further, acrimony persists between the teacher and the taught, and among neighbours. Hence the moot question is how an individual can improve his AQ score, ie., his Acceptability Quotient, so that he becomes unconditionally acceptable everywhere and to everyone.

The solution is perhaps simple; the finest human qualities of an understanding mindset, unconditional readiness to alleviate the pain of others (including the nearby fauna) with compassion, and the willingness to treat the surrounding nature with responsibility, as already said in the beginning, determine a person's AQ levels. And a person with liberal amounts of these qualities is indeed accepted everywhere and by everyone! As further said, fortunately, only attitudinal changes are required to raise one's AQ levels.

Let's now refocus on the distinct line that demarcates intelligence from wisdom, which is the core theme of this article.

During our day-to-day activities, we may have noticed that wisdom rules the roost compared to the intelligence levels of people. While wisdom is impulsive, and thus builds bridges between people bringing them closer without any inhibitions, intelligence, on the other hand, often carrying a mountain of ego with it, erects both visible and invisible barriers between people. Wisdom, coming with maturity, modesty, and born out of years of experience, ensures that an individual remains *a part* of the group, whereas intelligence, placing a false aura of superiority around an individual, keeps him *apart* from the group (though we may not rule out exceptions). This may be the reason why wisdom finds ready acceptability everywhere, by which we may safely infer that wisdom raises one's AQ levels.

Following incident that happened in a corporate office as recently compiled from the electronic media aptly highlights the attitude of the intelligentsia.

A large corporate office hung a board at its premises with the following message: "If you look at this board and stroke your chin, you may appear intelligent and cultured." Nearly all people who looked at the board immediately stroked their chins!!

The above incident shows that the intelligentsia is more concerned about what the outside world would think about it and is highly influenced by external forces, rather than by its own innate qualities, and is gripped by fear psychosis and quite often succumbs to pressures, both external and internal.

In my further quest for knowing more about the characteristics that differentiate intelligence from wisdom, I have made some honest attempts to delve deeper into the subject and stumbled upon certain fascinating facts and exhaustive information during my widespread search, a perusal of which would reveal how strikingly these two traits differ from each other. Here go the facts:

1. Intelligence leads to arguments; wisdom leads to settlements

2. Intelligent man thinks he knows; wise man knows he thinks

3. Intelligence is the power of will; wisdom is power over the will

4. Intelligent man is wordy; wise man is worldly

5. Intelligent man talks to keep the conversation going; wise man speaks to keep the conversation enriching

6. Intelligence is heat, it burns; wisdom is warmth, it comforts.

7. Intelligence is the pursuit of knowledge; it tires the seeker. Wisdom is the pursuit of truth; it inspires the seeker.

8. Intelligent man wants to control the flow; wise man goes with the flow

9. Intelligent man is always insistent; wise man is ever consistent

10.   Intelligence is holding on; wisdom is letting go.

11.   Intelligence leads; wisdom guides.

12.   Intelligent man thinks there is nothing to learn after a stage; wise man knows there is always something to learn after every stage.

13.   Intelligent man always tries to prove his point; wise man well thinks whether there really is a point.

14.   Intelligent man intrudes; wise man accommodates.

15.   Intelligent man freely gives unsolicited advice; wise man keeps his counsel until all options are considered.

16.   Intelligent man understands what is being said; wise man understands what is left unsaid.

17.   Intelligent man speaks out of turn; wise man waits for his turn.

18.   Intelligent man sees everything as relative; wise man sees everything as related.

19.   Intelligent man preaches; wise man reaches.

20.   Some people are wise; some otherwise!!

Above are only a few glaring observations differentiating these two traits. Several great personalities born on this planet during the past 3 centuries, and those born even before the Common Era, and great texts written from time immemorial have shed far more light in this context, perusal of which would reveal that the quotes and texts contained a profound insight in them...

William Wordsworth (1770-1850): Underlining the proximity existing between modesty and wisdom, Wordsworth, one of the greatest English Poets, reasons that wisdom is oftentimes nearer when we stoop than when we soar.

Bertrand Russell (1872-1970): Defining wisdom as a five-fold concept comprising personal gaining of knowledge, understanding, experience, discretion, and intuitive understanding, Russell, a great British philosopher, mathematician, logician, and Nobel Laureate, said that wisdom is the capacity to apply these qualities well towards finding solutions to problems and continued to say: *"wisdom is the judicious and purposeful application of knowledge that is valued in society."*

According to Russell, who was vastly regarded as a public intellectual, historian, and social critic, comprehensiveness mixed with a sense of proportion, full awareness of the goals of human life, understanding, and impartiality are the four factors that constitute wisdom. Out of all these factors, Russell further says, the essence of wisdom essentially lies in impartiality. A couple of Russell's quotes on wisdom vis-à-vis intelligence may be certainly more appropriate here:

- *So far as I can remember, there is not one word in the Gospels in praise of intelligence*

- *Fear is the main source of superstition and one of the main sources of cruelty. To conquer fear is the beginning of wisdom*

In Chapter VII (Can a Scientific Society be Stable) of his vastly read and well-regarded book ***The Impact of Science on Society***, Russell warns: *"Broadly speaking, we are in the middle of a race between human skill as to means and human folly as to ends. Given sufficient folly as to ends, every increase in the skill required to achieve them is to the bad. The human race has survived hitherto owing to ignorance and incompetence; but, given knowledge and competence combined with folly, there can be no certainty of survival. Knowledge is power, but it is power for evil just as much as for good. It follows that, unless men increase in wisdom as much as in knowledge, increase of knowledge will be increase of sorrow."*

Albert Einstein (1879-1955): Describing wisdom as the intuitive mind and intelligence as the rational mind and comparing wisdom to a sacred gift while relegating intelligence to the position of a faithful servant, the German-born theoretical physicist, and Nobel Laureate says: *"We have created a society that has forgotten the gift but honours the servant!"* Again, according to Einstein, who was widely acknowledged as the greatest physicist of all times, while an intelligent person solves a problem, a wise man altogether avoids it in the first place!!

Harivansh Rai Bachhan (1907-2003): Differentiating between information and knowledge, and knowledge and wisdom, Harivansh Rai Bachhan, an Indian poet, and writer of the *Nayi Kavita* literary movement of the 20th Century Hindi literature, best known for his work *"Madhushala,"* and a Padma Bhushan awardee in 1976 for his service to Hindi literature, says: *"The kind of knowledge gained through good education is just more than the acquisition of information. Knowledge is learning what to do with all that information. And learning what to do with knowledge is the path to wisdom."*

Sri Sathya Sai Baba (1926-2011): Emphasizing that wisdom is the starting step to acquiring permanent peace, Sathya Sai Baba, the Indian spiritual leader said: *"Open the gates of wisdom, tear the veil of ignorance, enter the abode of Divine Bliss, and rest in peace forever."*

Stephen William Hawking (1942-2018): The English theoretical physicist, cosmologist, author, and director of research at the Centre for Theoretical Cosmology at the University of Cambridge had said: *"People who boast about their IQ are losers"* and continued: *"it is not clear that intelligence has any long-term survival value."* Hawking, considered as one of the most brilliant scientists with an unparalleled IQ level, and who at the age of 21 suffered from ALS (Amyotrophic Lateral Sclerosis), a serious motor neuron disease, continued to live with the very severe nervous disability for 55 years till his death at the age of 76 in March 2018, did his research while being confined to the wheelchair. His statements reveal the 'importance' the genius had attached to the intelligence factor of humans!

Dr. Erol Ozan: *A* professor in information technology at the East Carolina University, whose research projects have been sponsored by various prestigious organizations including NASA and the National Science Foundation of the USA, and currently based in Raleigh, North Carolina, Ozan emphasizes that *"intelligence without wisdom brings destruction."*

Nathaniel Adebesin: Currently founder & Director, New Lead Innovation, Nigeria, and an experienced planner with a demonstrated history of working in the professional training & coaching industry, Adebesin says *"Wisdom and Intelligence are different; the places wisdom will take you; intelligence is too shallow to even think about them."*

Dr. T.P. Chia: Saying that wisdom is more than knowledge, intelligence, and experience combined, Chia, Singapore's rebel leader, and a 2015 Nobel Prize Nominee sums up that wisdom is the combination of good sense, understanding, insightful judgment, and brilliant farsightedness. He further says: *"wisdom is the mother of kindness, temperance, and tolerance."* Chia, a teacher, and Physics lecturer, later a Ph. D in development economics, and a former MP, was imprisoned for 23 years for allegedly conducting pro-communist activities against the Government of Singapore. Dr. Chia was the second-longest serving prisoner of conscience after the late Nelson Mandela. He then went on to spend 9 more years under severe restrictions, which makes his total length of incarcerations and restrictions longer than what Mandela had endured.

Edmund Burke: The Irish statesman, economist, and philosopher, who served as a member of the British Parliament, Burke says, *"Never, no, never did nature say one thing and wisdom say another."*

A.R. Rehman: The outstanding Indian music maestro, Rehman, outlining that wisdom comes from within and that knowledge needs to be acquired from outside, says knowledge sometimes puts a screen on one's wisdom and cautions one to ensure that one's intelligence or knowledge does not become a barrier to one's wisdom.

Anthony (Tony) Douglas Williams: The Canadian writer, and author in his book ***Inside the Divine Pattern,*** says: *"knowledge comes from learning, while wisdom comes from living"* and continues: *"our words and actions reflect our wisdom."* Stating that we all will be rich when humanity measures wealth by love, truth, and wisdom, Douglas exhorts that this is the way to find peace. His studies are now found to have a link with recent scientific discoveries. The words and wisdom of Williams are as profound today as they were when his book was first published in 2007. His spiritual writings express his affinity with truth, and he is passionately in love with all humanity and the animal kingdom.

Ratan Tata: Greatly emphasizing on the essential need to lead a life with humanistic impulse, and exhorting that all humans are not humane, Ratan Tata, the Chairman Emeritus of Tata Sons, said in his widely acclaimed quote filled with imposing wisdom: *"There is a lot of difference between human being and being human – A few understand it!"*

Confucius (551 BCE-479 BCE): Considered the quintessence of Chinese sages during the 6th Century BCE, Confucius, placing wisdom, compassion, and courage on the highest pedestal of mankind said these three traits constitute the universally recognized moral qualities of men.

Socrates (470 BCE – 399 BCE): The classical Greek Philosopher from Athens credited as the founder of Western Philosophy and among the first moral philosophers of the ethical tradition of thought beautifully differentiated intelligence from wisdom from his own point of reference. While saying that he knew he was intelligent because he knew that he knew nothing, Socrates concluded that *"The only true wisdom is knowing you know nothing!"*

Chanakya (375 BCE-283 BCE): The ancient Indian philosopher, economist, royal advisor, and master political strategist, also known as Kautilya and Vishnugupta, and best known for his enormous wisdom, Chanakya was singularly successful in helping Chandragupta rise to power and thus in the establishment of the vast Mauryan Empire. He is regarded as a great thinker and diplomat in modern India for his sheer wisdom and is referred to as the Indian Machiavelli as a result of his undisputed and shrewd techniques and policies, which mirror a "realist" approach to politics, diplomacy, and warfare.

His famous *Arthashastra*, the ancient political treatise dating back to the 4th century BCE, reflected his great wisdom, which led many Indian nationalists to regard him as one of the earliest people who envisioned a united India spanning the entire subcontinent. His second text *Chanakyaniti*, also known as *Chanakya Neeti Shastra*, written during the same period, is a collection of aphorisms and served as a moral guide to the emperor.

The diplomatic enclave in New Delhi is named Chanakyapuri in his honour. Institutes named after him include Training Ship Chanakya of the Indian Maritime University (Navi Mumbai), Chanakya National Law University (Patna), and Chanakya Institute of Public Leadership (Mumbai). Chanakya circle in Mysuru has been also named after him.

Epicurus (341 BCE-270 BCE): The Greek Philosopher from the 4th Century BCE, comparing wisdom to the health of the soul, says: *"Let no one be slow to seek wisdom when he is young, nor weary in search of it when he has grown old. For no age is too early or too late for the health of the soul."*

Marcus Aurelius (121 CE-181 CE): The emperor of Rome during the 2nd Century CE, and the last in the line of five good emperors known to have ruled Rome with authority, humanity, and competence and widely known as the philosopher-king, Marcus says: *"Take a good hard look at people's ruling principle, especially of the wise, what they run away from and what they seek out"*, which clearly explains that it's wisdom that has the ability to differentiate the grain from the chaff, meaning what to take and what not to, in life. Marcus further continues: *"Natural ability with education has more often raised a man to glory and virtue, than education without natural ability,"* which sums up his view on education (intelligence), in the absence of natural ability (wisdom). Under Marcus Aurelius, the Roman empire was guided by virtue and wisdom. His journal "*Meditations*" is a landmark of Stoic philosophy that has guided both powerful and common men and women for thousands of years and stands relevant even today, even 2000 years after it was first written.

Saint Augustine (354 CE-430 CE): Theologian and philosopher from Roman North Africa during the 4th Century CE, Augustine, stating that wisdom is never in harmony with haste, implying that decisions made in haste are devoid of wisdom, says: *"patience and wisdom are companions."*

Sri Adi Shankara (700 CE-750 CE): The 8th Century CE born great Indian Philosopher, Saint, and Vedic Scholar, while reportedly commenting about maturity (another synonym for wisdom) in human beings says: *"Maturity is when we stop trying to change others and instead focus on changing ourselves. Maturity is our ability to stop proving to the world how intelligent we are. Maturity is understanding everyone is right in his own perspective and accepting people as they are. Maturity is our ability to differentiate between needs and wants and letting go of our wants."* Finally, Adi Shankara says maturity is stopping attaching happiness to material things.

By close observation of the above comment offered by Sri Adi Shankara on maturity, it may be inferred that wisdom and maturity are interconnected, and whatever was stated by the great Indian saint about maturity equally applied to wisdom.

Citing a few very interesting quotes by some other great men of our own era which further emphasize the value of wisdom over intelligence, may be apt here. Here go the immortal quotes:

> *A loving heart is the truest wisdom - **Charles Dickens, the English Writer & social critic (1812-1870)***

> *Where is the life we have lost in living? Where is the wisdom we have lost in knowledge? Where is the knowledge we have lost in*

*information? - **T.S. Eliot, the American Playwright & one of the 20th Century's major poets (1888-1965)***

> *Knowledge comes, but wisdom lingers - **Alfred Lord Tennyson, the English Poet Laureate (1809-1892)***

> *Knowledge speaks, but wisdom listens - **Jimi Hendrix, the American musician, and songwriter (1942-1970)***

Apart from the above, a couple of anonymous quotes may also be worth citing here:

> *"Intelligence without wisdom is nothing more than stupidity that looks smart"*

> *"Knowledge is realizing the street is one way. Wisdom is looking both directions anyway"*

As stated in a beautiful article that appeared on the 'quartz.com' website, the difference between intelligence and wisdom is subtle but potent. According to the author of the article **Zat Rana**, *"while intelligence gives specific utility, wisdom inspires flexible versatility."*

The hilarious tales about wisdom surrounding **Tenali Rama** from the Court of the Vijayanagara Emperor Krishna Deva Raya (1471-1529) of the Tuluva Dynasty and those related to **Birbal** from the court of Akbar (1542-1605) need no special mention. The supreme and worldly wisdom exhibited by Krishna Deva Raya's Prime Minister, advisor, and guide, **Timmarasu**, in the day-to-day administration of the kingdom as well as in winning strategic battles for his emperor against the empire's arch enemies, at times without bloodshed, was etched in the pages of history.

The ancient Indian texts, **The Mahabharata,** and **The Ramayana** (estimated to have been compiled during the 5th & 7th Centuries BCE respectively) are two eternal works with boundless wisdom and values.

While the Mahabharata is the longest epic poem ever written with over one lac *shlokas* and long prose passages, a total seemingly consisting of about 1.8 million words (which was reportedly considered to be roughly ten times the combined length of Iliad and the Odyssey - the Greek epic poems dating back to the 8th and 11th Centuries BCE respectively), the Ramayana is roughly 1/4th of the size of the Mahabharata with 24,000 verses.

Several instances that depict wisdom while dealing with different situations can be traced to these two magnificent Hindu texts. The *Vidura Neeti & Yaksha Prashnalu* from the Mahabharata are two classic examples in this context, whereas the *Bhagavad Gita*, the 700-verse central part of Mahabharata, is the ultimate storehouse of all worldly wisdom, as testified by several great personalities across the globe.

Vidura, known for his dutifulness, impartial judgment, and steadfast dharma (righteousness), is considered the personification of the inner consciousness of the Mahabharata. *Vidura-neeti*, or Vidura's Statecraft, appearing in the Mahabharata's *Udyoga Parva* in the form of a dialogue between Vidura and King Dhritrashtra, is considered in some ways the forerunner to Chanakyaneeti, which had unfolded during the reign of Chandragupta Maurya during the 4th Century BCE.

Yaksha Prashnalu, or, the questions by *Yaksha* (*Yama Dharma*), constitute the approximately more than 100 questions posed to *Yudhishtara*, who was regarded as the quintessence of truth, and embodiment of wisdom. The questions were so varied that they ranged in content and depth from metaphysics to philosophy to several other subjects, and the answers given to each and every question by *Yudhishtara* were to the complete satisfaction of the *Yaksha*. This massive question-answer session, known as the *Dharma-Baka Upakhyan*, or Legend of the virtuous crane, appears in the *Aranya Parva* of the Mahabharatha. The unparalleled wisdom Yudhishtara possessed and exhibited while answering all the extremely difficult & crafty questions had not only won over the heart of the Yaksha but also in Yudhishtara getting all his four younger brothers back to life, who had lost their lives earlier due to their arrogance.

The Bhagavad Gita, the philosophical magnum opus of unrivalled meaning, deep insight, extraordinary brilliance, and zenith of all wisdom, is a dialogue between Krishna and Arjuna right before the start of the climactic Kurukshetra War and perhaps, the Gita is the only religious text that primarily deals with work ethics. At that crucial moment when Arjuna was supposed to take on the enemy with all fervour, seeing his own kith and kin and revered teachers in the opposite camp, and gripped in a moral dilemma on the rationale of war and on the choices before him vis-à-vis the right things to do, he drops his bow, and wonders if he should renounce and just leave the battlefield. The deep wisdom contained in the complete answers provided by Krishna to all of Arjuna's questions lifts him from the profound despair and doubt and prepares him back to perform his duty.

According to *Flood* (translator & scholar of Hinduism at Oxford University) and *Martin* (award-winning poet and translator at the City University of New York), although the *Gita* is set in the context of a war epic, the narrative is structured to apply to all situations; it wrestles with questions about *"who we are, how we should live our lives, and how should we act in the world."*

What several great men across the globe had opined or said about the *Bhagavad Gita* sums up its supreme importance and ingenious relevance, and unfolds the fathomless wisdom it eternally carries:

> ➢ *Ralph Waldo Emerson (1803-1882), American Essayist, Philosopher, and Poet:* *"I owed a magnificent day to the Bhagavad Gita. It was the first of books; it was as if an empire spoke to us, nothing small or unworthy, but large, serene, consistent, the voice of an old intelligence which in another age and climate had pondered and thus disposed of the same questions which exercise us."*

> ➢ *Swami Vivekananda (1863-1902):* According to Swami Vivekananda, *sva-dharma* in the *Gita* does not mean *"caste*

duty", rather it means the duty that comes with one's life situation (mother, father, husband, wife) or profession (soldier, judge, teacher, doctor, etc). For Vivekananda, the *Gita* was an egalitarian scripture that rejected caste and other hierarchies.

➤ ***Mahatma Gandhi (1869-1948)***: *"When doubts haunt me, when disappointments stare me in the face, and I see not one ray of hope on the horizon, I turn to the Bhagavad Gita and find a verse to comfort me; and I immediately begin to smile in the midst of overwhelming sorrow."*

➤ ***Sri Aurobindo (1872-1950), Indian philosopher, Yoga Guru, Poet, and Nationalist****: "The Bhagavad-Gita is a true scripture of the human race, a living creation rather than a book, with a new message for every age, and a new meaning for every civilization."*

➤ ***Hermann Hesse (1877-1962), the German-Swiss poet, novelist & Nobel Laureate****: "The marvel of the Bhagavad Gita is its truly beautiful revelation of life's wisdom which enables philosophy to blossom into religion."*

➤ ***Albert Einstein (1879-1955)***:

- *When I read the Bhagavad Gita and reflect on how God created this universe, everything else seems so superfluous*

- *I have made the Bhagavad Gita as the source of my inspiration and guide for the purpose of scientific investigation and the formation of my theories*

➤ ***Aldous Huxley (1894-1963), English Writer****: "The Bhagavad-Gita is the most systematic statement of spiritual evolution of endowing value to mankind. It is one of the clearest and most comprehensive summaries of perennial philosophy ever* *revealed; hence its enduring value is subject not only to India but to all of humanity."*

➢ *J. Robert Oppenheimer (1904-1967), Father of the Atomic Bomb*: *"Now I am become Death, the destroyer of worlds"*, after the Trinity Test of the Manhattan Project, which was the first detonation of a nuclear weapon, recalling the verses from the Bhagavad Gita.

Other great men across the globe who were deeply inspired by The Bhagavad Gita include our own missile man, Dr. APJ Abdul Kalam (1931-2015); the American Poet and essayist, T.S. Eliot (1888-1965); the Anglo-American novelist, Christopher Isherwood (1904-1986); the Swiss Psychiatrist and psychoanalyst, Carl Jung (1875-1961); the Turkish politician, poet, writer, scholar, and journalist and four times Prime Minister of Turkey between 1974 and 2002, Bulent Ecevit (1925-2006); and the American naturalist, essayist and poet, Henry David Thoreau (1817-1862), amongst several others.

The Ramayana, another Indian classic text of eternal value, is interspersed with teachings on the goals and purpose of human life. Its most important moral influence was the significance of virtue in the life of a citizen and in the ideals of the formation of a state or a functioning society. The instances related to i). Rama's paramount advice to his brother Bharatha, when the latter comes to the forest and urges Rama to return to the kingdom and establish his rule, in line with their departed father's ardent wish, ii). Vibheeshana's sagely advice to his own brother Ravana, when the latter captured Sita, and iii). Rama's instructions to Laxmana to learn from the same Ravana when the latter was on the verge of death lying in the battlefield, all glorify the value of wisdom in the fittest possible words. The Ramayana contains several such instances loaded with wisdom and virtues throughout.

Panchatantra, the collection of classic Indian interrelated animal fables in Sanskrit verse and prose written by Vishnusarma and roughly dating back to 200 BCE, is so popular across the world for its sheer wisdom that there is a version of *Panchatantra* in nearly every major language of India, and in addition, there are 200 versions of the text in more than 50 languages around the world. Its narrative illustrates, for the benefit of three ignorant princes, the central principles of prudent worldly conduct, or "the wise conduct of life."

Thirukkural, written by saint poet Thiruvalluvar over 2,000 years ago in the great age of Tamil Sangam literature, is another classic text that contains concise teachings on virtues. The text structured into 133 chapters (each chapter containing 10 couplets and each couplet 7 words), is a collection of total of 1330 couplets on moral teachings. Divided into three books on virtue (*aram*), wealth (*porul*), and love (*inbam*), the text is considered one of the greatest works on ethics and morality and is known for its universality.

This is one text that was oft quoted by Dr. A.P.J. Abdul Kalam for its immortal wisdom. There was always a delightful mention of this great work in all his books by Dr. Kalam. In his 2015 publication, ***"The Guiding Light"***, which was an inspirational selection of quotations by him that have influenced and shaped his thinking, Kalam says: *"One book that has been almost like a code for living for me is the **Thirukkural**, which consists of couplets or **kurals**. Each of these contains profound truth or moral code, expressed in a few words but enfolding astonishing wisdom within it. There has been hardly any moment of conflict or despair in my life that the **Thirukkural** has not helped me to resolve."*

A couplet from the Thirukkural on the significance of wisdom with which Chapter 6 (The Knowledge Society) of Dr. APJ Abdul Kalam's other vastly read book *"The Ignited Minds: Unleashing the Power within India"* begins, may be very relevant here in the context of the supreme value the above great text places on wisdom. The couplet says: *"Wisdom is a weapon to ward off destruction; It is an inner fortress which enemies cannot destroy."*

Tao Te Ching, the 4th Century BCE short treatise of Chinese origin says: *"Wisdom always leads to truth, while intelligence may be used to deceive."* This Chinese Classical Text, traditionally credited to the sage Lao Tzu (also rendered as Laozi and Lao-Tze, an ancient Chinese philosopher and writer), continues to emphasize that *"knowing others is intelligence; knowing yourself is wisdom; mastering others is strength, mastering yourself is true power."*

NIV (New International Version) Bible, with its origins spanning to the original texts written in Hebrew (the Old Testament; period ranging from 8th/7th Centuries BCE to 2nd/1st Centuries BCE) & Greek (the New Testament; period ranging from 3rd/1st Centuries BCE to 16th Century CE), says fools despise wisdom and instruction. Stating that an intelligent heart acquires knowledge, while the ear of the wise seeks knowledge, the NIV Bible says wisdom is far more valuable than intelligence.

Wisdom is not about being smart, but about knowing how to act correctly in any given situation. *While intelligence may be fixed, we can increase wisdom.* The implication is that whereas IQ, like one's height and eye colour, may be relatively fixed, wisdom can be sought, learned, and increased. It would grow deeper and wider with age and experience. With every journey around the sun, ie., with each passing year, we would learn by experience regarding how better to look after ourselves and those around us, NIV Bible says.

Conclusion: The pre-eminence and acceptance of wisdom as a trait overriding intelligence is thus a matter of testimony to the fact that wisdom had always scored over intelligence from time immemorial as evidenced by the oldest ever revelations starting from what was mentioned in the ancient Indian, Chinese, Hebrew & Greek texts to what is being presently said and quoted during our very modern times. The continuation of the same position to date as testified by the observations of several great personalities across the globe during the past three centuries and much before, stated in the foregoing paragraphs, is proof that this invincible truth is ageless.

When something becomes the truth, it by default becomes universally acceptable. Wisdom, undisputedly bestowed with the zenith of AQ levels, thus finds ready acceptance everywhere and with everyone. The intelligentsia, on the other hand, still cocky about its so-called ever-high IQ levels, and wearing a false aura around it, is not ready yet in a big way to selflessly distribute the fruits of its knowledge to the deprived, and is struggling to find acceptability, with very low AQ levels.

The minuscule efforts by very few NGOs and very few individuals notwithstanding, even primary education is still not reaching the poor and the needy in the country in the way it is supposed to reach.

It's therefore of urgent need that, everyone who is a part of the educated intelligentsia, rises to the occasion by imbibing the *humanistic impulse* and the nation-building qualities and starts dissipating his knowledge to the nation's downtrodden, right earnest. As propounded by Swami Ranganathananda[*] it's time each and every fruit of science and

---

[*]   Born on 15th Dec 1908 in Trissur, Kerala, Swami Ranganathananda's maiden name was Shankaran Kutty. He was a Trustee of the Ramakrishna Math, a member of the Governing Body of the Ramakrishna Mission, and President of the Ramakrishna Math/Hyderabad, a position he had held for nearly two decades. He later became the 13th President of the Ramakrishna Math & Mission's Hq at Belur/West Bengal during September 1998 and remained so for 7 years till his demise in April 2005 at the age of 96.

Over the years he addressed large audiences across the globe on the spiritual and cultural themes. His thoughts revealed a penetrating mind in quest for attainment of man's development on these two important subjects. Swami Ranganathananda was noted for his contributions which formed a bridge between Science and Vedantic spirituality. He went on several world tours as an ambassador of religion and Indian culture, travelling to over fifty countries in North and South America, Asia, Africa, and Europe, including the then Communist states of USSR, Poland and Czechoslovakia.

technology reached the masses from the scientist and his laboratory. Having been educated at the expense of the State, it's the bounden responsibility of all the educated in this country to discharge their duty to the nation by selflessly coming forward to give back to the nation what it has given to them. This must be done with compassion and passion and without any strings attached. Then only the nation shall remember them as real human beings and their real value lies in doing so. Otherwise, they continue to run the risk of being labelled as traitors to the nation, as exhorted by Swami Vivekananda.

The need of the hour, therefore, is to acquire the *WISDOM* that is necessary to accomplish this humanistic task right away and in the right direction.

It's time to take this important decision NOW, and simultaneously act upon it by putting your heart and soul into it! Are You Ready To Do So?

--//--

He received the Indira Gandhi Award for National Integration in 1987 and the Gandhi Peace Prize in 1999, both of which were conferred on the Ramakrishna Mission, but later declined the Padma Vibhushan during 2000, as it was conferred on him in his individual capacity but not on the Mission.

11

Perils Of The 'Well-Being' Technology

Before delving deep into the subject, let's first make an honest attempt to understand what 'well- being' generally means. The Oxford English Dictionary defines 'well-being' as the state of being comfortable, healthy, or happy. Another authoritative source of the English language, the Collins English Dictionary, while describing 'well-being' as a good or satisfactory condition of existence, again adds that it is a state characterized by health, happiness, and prosperity. Yet another, the Merriam Webster's Dictionary, also defines 'well-being' as the state of being healthy, happy, and prosperous.

As can be seen from the commonalities found from the above respected sources of the English language, the phrase well-being is essentially related to the parameters of health, happiness, and prosperity. Out of these three factors, while the first and the third, viz., health and prosperity, primarily comprise the physical, and sociological dimensions of well-being respectively, the second factor, happiness, forming the pedestal on which well-being rests, is a psychological dimension. As such well-being per se is something that is related to the state of mind as well as body and hence is both *intangible* and *tangible* simultaneously. In view of the above position, it may hence be said that the experience or situation that emanates from the right mix of all these three factors, and which gives rise to good physical and mental health, high life social order, great satisfaction, a sense of meaning or purpose, and most importantly, a stress-free life, constitutes well-being.

With a view to scientifically analyze what actually represents the concept of well-being, the London-headquartered European Social

Survey (ESS) conducted a global study known as the *Multi-dimensional Psychological Well-being Survey (MPWS)*. The exercise involving approximately 2.4 lac individuals was carried out in 21 countries and spanned over 6 years from 2006 to 2012. Though it is almost a decade now since the above survey was completed, the findings of the survey have been found to be eternal in value and stand relevant even today and shall remain so in the future as well. Following are the major findings of the above global study...

> ➤ well-being is the combination of feeling good and functioning well

> ➤ well-being is the 'experience' of positive emotions such as happiness, contentment, development of one's potential, inculcation of discipline, and bringing in a sense of purpose in one's life

> ➤ the individuals high in well-being exhibited greater productivity at the workplace, and were found to have capacity for more effective learning, increased creativity, more prosocial behaviours, and building positive relationships

> ➤ well-being has been linked to success at professional, personal, and interpersonal levels

A perusal of the above findings would reveal that while the crux of well-being at the generic level is happiness and life satisfaction, it may well be said that the factors listed above constitute the natural extension of these two basic situations. ***Thus, we may finally conclude that 'well-being' is the state of a healthy mind and healthy body, governed and enveloped by the physical, sociological, and psychological dimensions of life, with built-in components of 'happiness' and 'satisfaction' that cannot be acquired from outside but need to be felt & found from inside.*** In view of this specific feature, well-being is just not confined to humans alone, but is relatable to everything that has life, i.e., the surrounding fauna and flora, too!

Coming to the technology part, well, it's an established fact that in the present age of science & technology and the associated development in the economic sense, which is hardly a couple of centuries old (just naught compared to the age of the earth, which is about 5 billion years), every single tangible thing that provides comfort and joy to humans is assumed as the source of their happiness, and thus accordingly labelled as the cause of their well-being. Though the benefit of penetration of science & technology in our lives, no doubt, is very big and significant, one should never forget the fact that unfortunately, these two specialties of learning have brought with them enormous perils as well, which have the potential to annihilate the entire life from the face of the earth, if put to wrong use. The present age has already been and still is a sad witness to the massive destruction science & technology had caused and are still causing to life on earth, whenever the scientific technique fell into the wrong and irresponsible hands. Distressingly we have already seen & are still seeing this terrible menace the world over.

In his widely read and acclaimed book *"The Impact of Science on Society"* first published 7 decades ago in 1952, *Bertrand Russell,* the British polymath, Nobel Laureate, philosopher, mathematician, logician, and social reformer, warns: *"Broadly speaking, we are in the middle of a race between human skill as to means and human folly as to ends. Given sufficient folly as to ends, every increase in the skill required to achieve them is to the bad. The human race has survived hitherto owing to ignorance and incompetence; but, given knowledge and competence combined with folly, there can be no certainty of survival. Knowledge is power, but it is power for evil just as much as for good. It follows that, unless men increase in wisdom as much as in knowledge, increase of knowledge will be increase of sorrow."*

The above observations of Russell found in Chapter VII (*Can a Scientific Society be Stable*) of his book are as relevant today as they were then. It may be noted that Russell meant science & technology whenever he mentioned knowledge and he had always wished that science & technology remain the domain of the right people, so that only the benefits, but not perils, arising out of the research and consequent application can be passed on to the people. A careful perusal of what Russell had said in his book would reveal that science and technology have the potential to cause damage in equal measure as benefits to society if they fell into the wrong hands (earlier reference made to the above book was in the article "Intelligence Vs Wisdom").

We are aware of the enormous benefits of electricity, the biggest gift of modern science, to the welfare of mankind. It's impossible to imagine modern life if access to electricity is denied, but the same electricity has the infinite potential to eliminate life if put to destructive use. Similar is the case with any scientific and technological innovation, right from a visibly innocuous pin to an airplane (can we forget the 9/11 attacks of 2001 carried out on the WTC using an airplane?), as all have dual effects. This underlines the fact that technology, however important & sophisticated it might be, can lead to the un-being of the people rather than the well-being of the people if passed into the control of polluted minds.

Man faces devastation when availability falls short of the requirement. Likewise, he faces devastation also when availability exceeds requirement as in the case of the explosive rise in certain natural occurrences at times. While rains are essential for the preservation of life, floods are not; sea waves are enjoyable as they bring in good breeze and joy and are necessary for harnessing tidal energy, but a tsunami is not. Similarly, the summer heat, the winter cold, and other vagaries of nature are welcome when in limited magnitude. Similar is the situation with fire; as long as fire remains our servant, we survive, and the moment it becomes our master, we perish. These simple examples underline the fact that beyond a certain limit everything, however good and essential it is, causes extreme harm. And technology is not an exception...

A healthy mind and a healthy body, which together constitute the precursor for the well-being of an individual, are dependent on 4 pillars, viz., i). good nutrition, ii). regular exercise, iii). adequate rest, and iv). great attitude, which are like the 4 legs of the 'chair of well-being' of an individual. Again, out of these 4 legs, great attitude constitutes the single intangible leg, which inspires and drives the remaining three tangible legs. In order to ensure that the 'chair of well-being' remains stable, all these 4 legs must be i). similar in strength and size, and ii). must be firmly attached to the chair. Else, it need not be emphasized what would happen to the chair!

Now, let's conduct a quick search to find out whether technology has any role in ensuring that the above two conditions are met so that the chair of well-being ever remains stable. Without much effort, our search would lead to an emphatic *'NO'*, since the concept of 'well-being' itself is bestowed with the in-built feature of immense inherent strength that flawlessly ensures fulfilment of the above two conditions, with technology playing zero role in the whole process.

A few examples may be relevant here in order to substantiate the above view. Even today people from several tribes across the globe remain unexposed to technology in any form, yet no one can belittle the state of their well-being from the perspective of the environment they live in. They do not have access to any modern gadgets, let alone modern medicine, yet they are far away from disease, leading healthy and happy lives. Even in our olden days, our forefathers lived within their available resources with no exposure to technology but led lives of great well-being. They were quite healthy, discharging their daily chores on their own, in the process typically ensuring continued sustenance of their health and well-being.

However, the above situation is clearly not the case in today's modern world, where there is easy access to technology in all possible forms, right from the time we are awake in the morning till the time we are back to sleep at night, and even after we are asleep.

What causes deep concern is the unwelcome invasion of technology today in several forms into almost every nook and corner of our lives, even into matters trivial. This has acquired further huge proportions especially after the advent of the internet. What is highly devastating is, blatant acceptance of technology and brazen (or helpless?) dependence on it by a vast majority of the people is rendering them infructuous, sluggish, and vulnerable to disease and loot, putting their well-being at a serious stake. One of the several glaring examples in this context is the flooding of several 'money' or 'game' apps and such similar traps on social media platforms, resulting in several people falling easy prey to those apps, in the process, losing heavily both on their health and wealth fronts. Not only this, sadly technology is making people lead secluded lives, even while staying together! People, in general, are taking recourse to technology at the slightest pretext, even for attending to their easy domestic, routine, and simple chores, neglecting their once prized physical labour, and are thus becoming victims to several lifestyle diseases. Further, today's age is a sad witness to the massive and endless hazards associated with other forms of modern technology called 'hacking', 'cyber fraud', etc.

On the other hand, in a welcome development, another set of people again in today's age, sensible to the perils of technology, are willingly keeping themselves away from it, and living and leading happy and exuberant lives of well-being, a fact, no one can deny. Hence, all said and done, a judicious thought process is needed while sourcing and using technology, i.e., where and when to embrace it and where and when to discard it.

As the old adage, "all that glitters is not gold" goes, all the so-called 'well-being' that is linked to technology is not the 'real' well-being, because technology is changing at the whiff of a wink, rendering yesterday's 'good' technology getting labelled 'bad' today, in view of the continuous discoveries that are bringing to light the ill-effects arising due to the rampant dependence on technology. Therefore, from a conventional viewpoint, while it may be claimed that technology is 'contributing' to the well-being of people, such a contribution may not be lasting long, unless it's honestly backed by a great attitude. Else, such a contribution would by default get converted into only retribution to people's well-being! Though the dash of 'well-being' experienced by people due to the limited use of technology is appreciable, the twin facts that i). the damage caused to people due to the continuous dependence on it has always been markedly high and, ii). its deliberate misuse is on a rapid rise, cannot be ignored.

This situation thus unequivocally stipulates that technology has **NO** decisive function whatsoever in either 'deciding' or 'defining' the well-being of people but may only be in 'furthering' the well-being of people, that too, in certain specific cases and again, when used sensibly. Hence it can be inferred that while great attitude and well-being succinctly co-exist, technology and well-being do not, in the absence of great attitude. As we have already seen, great attitude constitutes the single intangible leg out of the four legs of the chair of well-being that drives the other three tangible legs.

Thus, while some may still say that humans + technology = well-being, it can unquestionably be concluded that humans + technology + great attitude = well-being! Even where technology is around but a great attitude is **NOT** abound, there cannot be well-being, as asserted by Ruaaell* several decades ago. Hence do **NOT** err in concluding that the level of one's well-being is directly proportional to the level of access one has to technology. The call of the day, therefore, is to let technology remain your servant, but not the other way round! And you must not allow technology to override you...

It's time to take this important decision NOW, and simultaneously act upon it by putting your heart and soul into it! Are You Ready To Do So?

---

*   Russell was awarded the Nobel Prize in 1950 for literature in recognition of his varied and significant writings in which he championed humanitarian ideals and freedom of thought, and he received the award primarily for his anti-religious book, **"Marriage and Morals"**.

12

Hislop College – The Pride Of Central India

What was founded in 1846 by a Scottish Missionary, Rev Stephen Hislop (1817-1863), a noted evangelist, educationist, linguist, keen naturalist, and geologist, with just 30 students as a boys' school in old Nagpur, has turned out into Hislop College in 1883 after it is named after him. Since then, the College, already with 139 years of historical legacy, has grown by leaps and bounds and blossomed into one of the finest institutions of higher learning in Central India, offering many UG, PG, and doctoral programmes in Arts, Science and Commerce streams, effectively catering to the vast educational and research needs of the Nation, successfully rolling out more than 4000 students a year.

The oldest and most venerable institution of the region, Hislop College had initially started with a staff strength of one Principal (Rev. J.G. Cooper) and six professors at the time of its establishment in 1883 in the Mahal area of Nagpur. On 4 September 1863, its founder, the Rev Hislop, during the course of exploration, drowned in the Bori River near Takalghat (somewhere close to today's Umrer, about 30 Km from Nagpur) which caused his sad demise. The green mineral "Hislopite" is also named after him.

Though Nagpur was the Capital of the Central Provinces, the city did not have a college until 1882. Thanks to the untiring efforts of Rev. Stephen Hislop, who was determined to provide education to the downtrodden and subjugated of the region, the city has had the privilege of becoming a seat of great learning and education in the later years.

The History of Hislop College may be divided into three periods. The first period (1845-1883) begins with the arrival of Rev. Stephen Hislop in Nagpur in 1845 and the establishment of Anglo-vernacular schools. The second period (1883-1941) begins with the emergence of the college in 1883, aptly named after him. The Third period (1941 onwards) begins when the Foreign Mission Church of Scotland transferred the entire control and management of the college into the Indian Hands in 1941.

The college was initially affiliated to the University of Calcutta until 1904, and later to Allahabad University. In 1923 it was one of the six colleges affiliated to the University of Nagpur, which came into being 4 decades after the establishment of Hislop College. The college is enormously reputed in Nagpur and its surrounding areas and is one of the best places to study in Maharashtra. The College is well-known for academic excellence, and vivacious campus life and makes a strong contribution to the betterment of civic, social, and cultural life in the region. The College is blessed to have on its rolls a strong, dedicated, and committed faculty with an unflinching fortitude to mould the students for the better and give them a distinct shape in the field of their choice. The seven Graduate Attributes the college has defined reflect the keenness the faculty of the College has towards the students, and every student is expected to imbibe each one of them upon completion of a programme from the College.

Putting these attributes in a structured way, we can arrive at a beautiful expression that very aptly describes what the students are destined to become after they proudly walk out of the vast corridors of the College with the degrees they earned in their hands. I would like to coin the expression something like this: "The alumni/alumnae of Hislop College, after years of consistent toil, having matured into highly *resourceful and responsible* individuals, with *effective communication skills, ethical and moral values, investigative* and *critical thinking* capabilities, fortified with massive *reflective learning* ability that collectively made them the ultimate in their *domain knowledge,* strive to add value to the people whom they meet*!* The above seven words in italics & bold constitute the seven attributes the College expects to see in each of its students as they finally leave the college premises.

Run by the Hislop Education Society under the aegis of the Church of North India Synod, New Delhi, Hislop college is accredited with an 'A' grade and a score of 3.15 CGPA (Criteria-wise Grade Point Averages) on a four-point scale by the NAAC (National Assessment and Accreditation Council), an independent body of the UGC (University Grants Commission). An institutional CGPA on a four-point scale in the range of 3.01 to 4.00 denotes an 'A' grade, which means the performance of the college on all fronts has been consistently found to be 'Very Good'.

In 2009 the College celebrated its quasi-quincentennial anniversary, a historic milestone on completing 125 years. Hislop College is among the 19 Colleges across the country which were granted the Special Heritage Status in 2015 by the UGC. Only two other colleges from Maharashtra (St. Xavier's College in Mumbai and Fergusson College in Pune) had the rare distinction of being chosen for this honor. The alumni of Hislop College comprises a glittering galaxy of great personalities. Bharat Ratna Baba Amte and the 9th Prime Minister of India, P. V. Narasimha Rao were amongst the illustrious and rare jewels this college had produced (source: https://www.nagpurtoday. in/historic-moment-for-city-as-hislop-gets-heritage-tag/07060551).

Hislop College is not just an institution of higher learning, but an epitome of brilliance, a synonym for quality teaching, and has left a very distinct mark on society in the field of education combined with ethics. With 22 Departments (10 in Arts, 2 in Commerce, 9 in Science, and 1 in Physical Education Faculties), 4 Student Associations (Environment Cell, NSS, Rotaract Club, and Woman Empowerment Cell), and 4 Support Centres (Training & Placement Cell, Counselling Cell, Mentoring Cell, and Competitive Examination Guidance Cell), the College makes every effort to build in rare attributes into its students aimed at providing value-based education combined with critical skills.

Different internal checks and counter checks carried out through its IQAC - Internal Quality Assurance Cell, and SQAC - Students' Quality Assurance Cell, with "You, We and Hislop" as its catchphrase take care of the continuous improvement needs in the quality of academic as well as ethical education that are provided by the college. These special efforts by the College Management are keeping the college on a higher pedestal making it distinctly unique, taking it way ahead in the race to excellence, in the process dwarfing the other institutions in the region leaving them way behind. Last but not the least; the College equally excels in the field of sports as well, both indoors and outdoors, and houses a vast library. The Indian Postal Department released a commemorative stamp in 2018 in recognition of the continuous services the college has been rendering to the people of the country in the field of quality education.

Apart from the regular academic programmes the college offers, it is indeed praiseworthy to note that the college is also offering a couple of career-oriented courses in Floriculture and Mushroom Cultivation that have the capability to turn the students into entrepreneurs. Besides these courses, the short-term courses being offered in Self-development and Public Speaking, Communication skills and Personality Development, Practical Accounting and Taxation, and Statistical Methods, have the potential to empower the students making them competent to win in this decidedly competitive world. The twin courses of "Campus to Corporate" and 'Finance and Accounting for BPS' (Business Process Services) being organized in association with TCS (Tata Consultancy Services) are laudable efforts of the College, which has been declared as a Minority Institution by the National Commission for Minority Educational Institutions in July 2015. The PTA (Parent-Teacher Association) and HISAR (Hislop Institute of Social Action and Research) are exemplary platforms through which the essential social connection is firmly getting established, ensuring that the delicate balance between the teachers and the taught remains steady and ongoing.

"Improvement of the quality of life, environment, and society, by training youth to become agents of growth, innovation and change" as its Vision Statement, and "making students competent and competitive by imparting them with the 21st-century knowledge, skills, and attitude" as its Mission Statement, no wonder, the products of this amazing Institution, who have got and getting transformed into the finest citizens, are not only serving their motherland in a big way in many critical areas but leaving their distinct mark at the global level also, bringing laurels to the Nation. The trendsetting, innovative and exemplary ways of imparting knowledge under active implementation by the principal and faculty members of Hislop College, and the office bearers of the Hislop Education Society are laudable, which no doubt, shall take the College to further loftier heights and finally to the pinnacle of glory and success in the field of continuous education in the region.

The above ideals are needed to be adopted in a big way if every educational institution is to acquire a good name and fame. It would be a matter of immense delight if all the educational institutions irrespective of their location in the country, especially at the countryside, are made better places of learning of not only various career courses, but most importantly the ideals of life, on the lines of the Hislop College. For, education coupled with ethics and human values only has got the tremendous capacity to bring in a progressive change in society. So, the need of the hour is to scrupulously ensure absorption of this great culture, the Hislop culture, and work towards it in all facets of life, irrespective of the position you are in, come what may...

It's time to take this important decision NOW, and simultaneously act upon it by putting your heart and soul into it! Are You Ready To Do So?

--//--

REAL-LIFE STORIES

[On Consumer And Woman Power]

1

Consumer Power At Its Best

It was Sunday, the 2nd of August 2015, around 8.30 PM. Seven of us (family members and friends) visited the Arya Bhawan Hotel located in Burdi (next to Big Bazaar) in Nagpur, for dinner. We all made ourselves comfortably seated in the upstairs part of the restaurant and ordered seven *'deluxe thalis'*, costing Rs. 230/- each + taxes.

Slowly, the place was getting filled with foodies. The crackling sound of tables and chairs being adjusted by the hotel staff by pulling two adjacent tables together, and rearranging chairs to suit the new size of the joined tables in sync with the group number, and as desired by the visiting gourmet groups, the whole scene though a little gawky, was nevertheless enjoyable. After a while, the food was served, and we were relishing the great aroma of the hot cuisine. And we all became busy and in fact, we were competing with one another, satiating our taste buds & hunger pangs......

As we were halfway through the course of enjoying the great food, we felt a little uncomfortable as a certain odd smell emanating from the washrooms (maybe someone had left the washroom doors open), started slowly enveloping the restaurant, more particularly, the area, where we were seated. After a look to our left and then to our right, we could observe that other co-diners too were experiencing the same quantum of discomfort. However, no one raised the matter with the restaurant staff. As time passed, the discomfort only grew.

I was watching... whether the restaurant Staff or Manager would come forward to take care of the situation first by closing the washroom door, and then by spraying some room freshener in order to combat the stink, which had by then become sore, and wrapped part of the restaurant's upstairs area. No one turned up...neither there was any attempt by any of the restaurant staffers to respond to the situation. Perhaps, they are habituated to the stink....so I thought!

We finished the dinner 'somehow'. The staffer attending to us was prompt in presenting the bill to us. The bill read Rs. 1665/- and I kept the money inside the bill diary and before retreating to the staircase, approached the cashier and lodged the complaint, as I had already made up my mind that I should take the matter to the notice of the hotel management. Giving a terribly careless look, the cashier asked me to talk to the 'Chief Cashier' sitting downstairs. I walked down the stairs and met the Chief Cashier and repeated my complaint. He in turn asked me to speak to the 'Owner' of the hotel, who was fortunately present at that point in time in his cabin located at a distance of about 20 feet diagonally opposite to the Chief Cashier's kiosk. I walked up to the owner, and once again put forth my complaint and demanded the complaint book, so that I could register my complaint in black and white. He had 'listened' to what I had said and then walked to the upstairs portion of the restaurant to practically 'verify' the complaint, with a promise that he would return with the complaint book.

About ten minutes had passed by, and the 'Owner' did not turn up and I was standing near the Chief Cashier waiting for the owner to come down with the complaint book. Infuriated at the delay, I once again told the Chief Cashier to call the Owner with the complaint book. The Chief Cashier sent someone upstairs and in about 5 minutes, some other staffer came down with the 'complaint book' and I was aghast at the look of the so-called complaint book. Believe me, it was a mere long-size notebook, children use in schools, the first few pages torn, and on the next page written, "Complaint Book". Shocked at the look of the 'complaint book', I called the Owner and demanded to know from him what type of complaint book it was, informing him that the fate of my complaint too would be like the previous torn pages, if at all I did write my complaint in that "Complaint Book" and asked him to provide me a printed complaint book, instead. He said, that was the only complaint book he had, and if at all I wanted to write the complaint, I may write in the same book.

At his reply, my adrenaline levels rose a little higher and I told the owner to arrange for a refund of 30% of the bill amount as compensation for poor ambiance conditions prevailing in the restaurant, failing which he would have to face the consequences arising out of Consumer Power.

I told him in a clear voice that he doesn't have the right to charge me for deficiency of service, and I pointed out at the failure and wilful neglect of the hotel management in providing us with the right ambiance, which we were entitled to. I was firm in my resolve to demonstrate what Consumer Power was, and what a consumer can do if he/she was not happy with the services rendered by the service provider. I told him that he cannot take the consumers for granted. I was *assertive* to the core, but not *aggressive*. That time around I was working in the corporate office of the Nagpur-based Western Coalfields Ltd, and a few days before, I was one of the participants in the Leadership Development Programme conducted by our prized HRD Deptt, in which '*Assertiveness*' was one of the topics.

The owner did not budge an inch. He said: *"I am not going to give you even a 1% discount come what may...do whatever you want. No one else complained about the so-called stink. It is strange that only your group of seven smelt it."* With a fixed gaze, not blinking my eyes, and looking straight into his eyes, in a soft yet firm voice, I told him: *"then be ready to receive the summons from the consumer forum...the license of your hotel shall become liable for cancellation, very soon."*

Dumb struck at my resoluteness, the owner became speechless. Approximately two minutes might have passed in silence; to my big surprise, the owner instructed his chief cashier to refund the money in *full*, ie., Rs. 1665/- back to me which I had paid just about 20 minutes earlier, as I was anticipating only 30% refund!! Though I was still insisting on a refund of only 30% of the total bill amount as demanded by me earlier, the Chief Cashier put back the full amount into my hands. The Owner, while expressing his deep regrets at the real deficiency in service, told me: "Sir, you are our valuable customer. Pl. forgive us. We will not give any room for similar complaints in future. 30% discount towards compensation for the discomfort caused as desired by you, and the balance 70% towards compensation for my ignorant arrogance. Please visit us again".

I was pleased to the hilt at his words, wondering what would have caused him to quickly change his mind. Is it the Consumer Power at its best, which brought a diametrically opposite change in his attitude, for the better? For me, I felt happy. The person, who was rude and wrong initially, ventured to correct himself by admitting his shortcomings, and finally emerged as a responsible hotelier. I really admired the change in the attitude of the Owner. Though the amount involved was insignificant, I was determined to take up the matter with the hotel staff for the sake of principle, for the sake of protecting the consumers' rights... And the consumer lying inside me had won hands down! Kudos to the consumer power! Long live the consumer!!

What you should do if you are also stuck in a similar situation, or may be dealing with a different situation, involving a commercial transaction? Just raise your voice and show your consumer power. When you do not find things right, it's absolutely necessary that you raise your voice with resoluteness. This ensures restoration of the desired order in the systems which were earlier suffering from serious disorders, paving the way for the re-functioning of all those systems with stability and lawfulness for the benefit of not only you, but the future generations as well. And it's your major social responsibility.

It's time to take this important decision NOW, and simultaneously act upon it by putting your heart and soul into it! Are You Ready To Do So?

--//--

2

Sheroes Of Agra

*What excited me in Agra? Believe me, it was not the Taj...*It all happened at the beginning of the 3rd week of Oct 2015, precisely on 15th Oct 2015, when we visited Agra, located on the picturesque banks of the river Yamuna, and the seat of the Mughal Empire during the 16th and 17th Centuries. During the winter of 2015, ten of us (comprising my sisters' family of five, my cousin, and my family of four), embarked on an 11-day trip to Rajasthan, the State of the erstwhile composition of several princely states mainly under the Rajput Rule and U.P, the land of epics and ancient cities. As we were in Agra, what particularly excited me was **not** the Taj Mahal, but something altogether different...

How the thought came? Before proceeding further, I must tell you what compelled me to include Agra in our itinerary and what pulled me to visit that all-poignant place as we stepped into the city. It was sometime during the 2nd fortnight of Sept 2015 that I chanced upon a show on one of the TV channels (TV-9 in the Telugu language) one night around 9:30. The tone of the anchor was sounding rather brisk and exciting, as she was announcing about the telecast of a great coverage their channel had made a few days earlier - perhaps the first of its kind in many months. The programme was just about to be aired on the channel.

The telecast was about **SHEROES** - the '*she heroes*'. The Sheroes are the five acid attack survivors; the first had suffered the attack outrageously at the hands of her stepmother; second - horribly at the hands of a reckless, brutal, and mindless crook; third - disgustingly at the hands of her cousin; fourth - distressingly at the hands of her own husband; and fifth, the daughter of the fourth - shockingly at the hands of her own father. After knowing about particularly the last two, I felt deeply disturbed, for I failed to comprehend how a man could throw acid on the faces of his wife and daughter...

The coverage gave vivid details about the five Sheroes, how they were persecuted, how they took the inconceivable pain and suffering, faced society, and finally how they decided to start afresh by pushing their unimaginable trauma to the back of their minds, and bringing superordinate grit on their disfigured faces. With extraordinary courage and a steely resolve, the Sheroes walked with their scars and started a restaurant, aptly named "Sheroes' Hangout." The coverage ended with the anchor urging everyone who had watched the program not to miss visiting the Sheroes, whenever he/she happened to be in Agra.

The story was so inspiring, stirring, and moving that I decided to meet the sheroes, undoubtedly the real defeaters, who decided to take life head-on with full might, without confining themselves to the four walls of their houses, hiding their stained faces, like many. After watching the show and listening to the narration by the anchor and the acid victims themselves, I decided that I must visit the Sheroes' Hangout and meet them during our forthcoming tour...that was how Agra got included in our itinerary. And the timing was perfect...I had chanced upon the show about the Sheroes and within days thereafter, our trip was through!!

The Exciting moment: The exciting moment came on 15th Oct 2015 around 7 PM, when we were in the majestic presence of the Sheroes. Three of them - Dolly, Rupa, and Ritu – only were available and we sadly missed the other two, Geeta and Neetu, who were reportedly out somewhere. The amazing women who valiantly fought life's worst battle with an unbeatable attitude and amazingly recovered from the dreadful chemical burns with fortitude were in front of us. The brave women who proved themselves as real fighters had kindly agreed to speak to us. After a couple of minutes of conversation, we were shaking hands with them!! Our excitement reached a crescendo!

They are courageous, they are spirited, they are highly inspiring, and they are exemplary. The Sheroes are much ahead in real bravery and real courage that they would easily out beat the celluloid heroes who are known only for their 'reel' bravery and 'reel' courage!! They are the real superstars who are proud to walk with their scars unlike the 'reel' superstars, who will desist the idea of sporting an artificial scar even during their screen appearances!! A little info about the Sheroes and how they suffered the acid attacks may be relevant here:

1. *Dolly,* 15, suffered a brutal attack when she was 12 years old at the hands of a rogue double her age when she refused his advances. The attack completely destroyed her nasal tract, causing her a permanent breathing problem. Presently a dancer and student at the Hangout, Dolly wants to become a doctor.

2. *Rupa,* 22, suffered the acid attack at the hands of her stepmother. The attack left her with severe burns and disfigured her face to a great extent. Not losing her heart, Rupa subsequently got trained in fashion design and presently is a fashion designer at the Hangout.

3. *Ritu,* 20, suffered the attack at the hands of her cousin due to some property dispute. She suffered 90% burns on her face and 25% burns on her body. A volleyball player earlier, Ritu wants to pursue her sport.

4. *Geeta,* 38, suffered the acid attack at the hands of her rogue husband. Having survived the cruel attack and resolved to be on her own, Geeta joined the Hangout. Presently she is the kitchen manager at the Hangout.

5. *Neetu,* 23, is Geeta's daughter. She suffered the gruesome attack at the hands of her own father when she was barely three years old. The attack had left her with a completely disfigured face and very little vision. During the attack, Neetu's baby sister, barely a few months old, also suffered severe burns and succumbed to the attack a couple of weeks later. Neetu is presently a singer at the Hangout.

Now, about the Awesome Sheroes' Hangout: Five of us, myself, Teja, Kanthi (my two sons), Hima Bindu, (my niece), and Sandhya (daughter of Swapna, another niece of mine and sister of Hima Bindu), thoroughly enjoyed our exquisite interaction with them. In a short but swift interface that followed, they told us how they made up their minds to come out of the initial physical pain they suffered, the mental trauma they underwent, and how they stood up to the assault on them with courage and nerve. After going a little deeper into their story, we came to know how they started their own enterprise, very aptly named *SHEROES' HANGOUT*, which is a living example of their determination not to succumb to the so-called fate, but to rise and stand-up, and face the life up-front, thereby showing to the whole world what woman-power means.

Sheroes' Hangout is an initiative by the "Stop Acid Attacks" (SAA) campaign that was founded in New Delhi in 2013. The Hangout was launched on 10 Dec 2014, World Human Rights Day. Since the day of its launch, Sheros' Hangout has been attracting international notice, as the survivors, instead of surrendering to hopelessness or isolation, and overcoming their initial hesitation to move out openly, are now working in the cafe and serving foreign tourists as well, with a lot of dignity, poise, and confidence, bringing more and more glory not only to them but to the walled city of Agra, which symbolizes eternal beauty and love!! Sheroes' Hangout is the first and only restaurant till probably a couple of years ago, to be opened, managed, and run by acid attack survivors.

Activities at Sheroes' Hangout: The activities of Sheroes are wide and varied. The hangout is a place to savor a coffee and satiate your hunger of both mind and belly. The hangout has a very nice Cafeteria with a wide variety of menu for the belly and a well-lined-up library with a wide diversity of books for the mind. Besides, it has a wonderful radio hub too with a wi-fi facility and an exhibition-cum-sale point of different items crafted by the brave women themselves. One unimaginable thing about the Sheroes' Hangout is, *"you eat and drink what you want, and pay* *as you wish.*" Believe me; the Hangout does not have a price board, only a menu board! Whoever visit the Café in the Sheroes' Hangout, mind their appetite, but not their pocket, i.e., they cautiously eat but liberally pay!! And the Hangout pays back in full measure what it receives... it extends stunning customer service that includes, amongst other things, a free reading time, as well as a free wi-fi facility without any bar on time, to all those who visit the premises. The Hangout also houses:

1. An "Activism Workshop" (where girls are trained free of cost on how to use computers and other gadgets helping them to utilize social media. Besides, programs on legal awareness, judicial procedure, etc., are conducted at the hangout on a regular basis) and

2. A "Handicrafts & Exhibition Space" (where many other acid survivors in the country can come, exhibit their products for sale, and perform their skills, again all for free). The walls of the cafe proudly display poses of the acid survivors in designer wear. Traditional Indian wicker furniture gives the café a pleasant ambiance. One corner houses a collection of books with a feminist theme - understandable given the injustice these women have suffered most at the hands of men.

Mesmerized by the idea behind running the Hangout by the 'stars with scars' and inspired by the service the Hangout is providing, many people wake up the philanthropist sleeping inside them and make sizable contributions to the Sheroes' Hangout. And the Sheroes keep only that much which is required to make them self-sustaining. The rest, they spend on the rehabilitation of other acid victims... They are very happy with this equation, they proudly say.

Our experience at The Sheroes' Hangout was wonderful and our interaction with the Sheroes was awe-inspiring. *I have found the Sheroes more beautiful than the Taj...*Can anyone afford to miss the real stars with scars while on a visit to Agra? I urge everyone who reads this real-life story to visit Sheroes' Hangout whenever she/he happened to be in Agra.

Comments from the social media: Extracts from a few comments and feedback reports on Sheroes' Hangout, compiled from the different social media platforms are re-produced below, which are a big testimony to the wide recognition and very high appreciation the Sheroes had earned over the less than a year since the existence of their inspiring venture:

Quote:

i.   *The new wave of feminism evolves at the Hangout through critical issues that cripple women and devoid them of equal opportunities. The irony is, such issues are abundant in South-Asian cultures, and it is this irony that pushed our Sheroes to set this Hangout here, in the city that boasts of the monument of love.*

ii. *As the idea of this space has evolved from a campaign for acid attack survivors, the ideas of beauty and the importance of appearance in society remain the epicenter of discussions and programmes run from here.*

iii. *You do need to munch when chilling out with friends. And revolutions, too, are not brought out with an empty belly. So, a tiny café serves delicious bites around the hour, along with some impressive beverages. The hangout also houses an ever-growing library (through contributions); so, pick your read, before you take the table.*

iv. *Campaigning for victims of acid attacks helped us realize that most of them come from a background where education is still limited to learning the basics of reading and writing. Using a computer or a mobile phone to connect and create still remains out of reach for many young girls being brought up in miserable circumstances throughout the country. The activism workshops at Sheroes' Hangout are aimed at training girls to use computers and other gadgets and helping them utilize social media as a real tool of empowerment and outreach. Programmes based on basic legal awareness, judicial and political procedures, cinema, art & culture, and gender issues keep the workshops engaging and lively.*

v.   *While the handicraft work of our Sheroes is always on display at the Hangout for sale, the exhibition space will provide a venue to many others in the country to come and exhibit/perform their skills. The idea is to organize gatherings like poetry and book readings, jewelry, and other design exhibits to engage Sheroes in a constructive activity while generating funds also to run this space.*

vi.   *Five acid attack victims, five incredible stories of lives shattered, but refusing to break. At Sheroes, the ideas of beauty and the importance of appearance are often the talking points. In a beauty-obsessed world, where women have found it hard to earn a livelihood, Sheroes' Hangout is an idea to show the world what they have been losing so far.*

Unquote:

On a perusal of the above quotes, we can understand the strong, strapping, and insightful imprints the Sheroes have left on people across the world and the worldwide recognition the Sheroes have received. As well said in the last quote above, their stories are incredible and their determination to refuse to break is simply astounding!!

A few Pictures and a Video: I place below a few file photos compiled from different social media platforms and the picture we had taken with Dolly, Rupa, and Ritu, and provide the link to a small video clipping showing our exciting interaction with them at their own place which we have found *holier than the so-called heaven!!*

We took the picture and shot the video with them with their kind permission... (Link to the video Clipping: https://youtu.be/ nMGPH9c7rC8)

Pic 1:

Our unforgettable picture with the Sheroes! From Left to Right: Kanthi, Teja, **Dolly, Rupa,** Sandhya, Hima Bindu, Me and **Ritu...**

Pic 2:

Sheroes' Hangout from outside: **Geeta** standing (file photo) ... (Geeta is Neetu's mother)

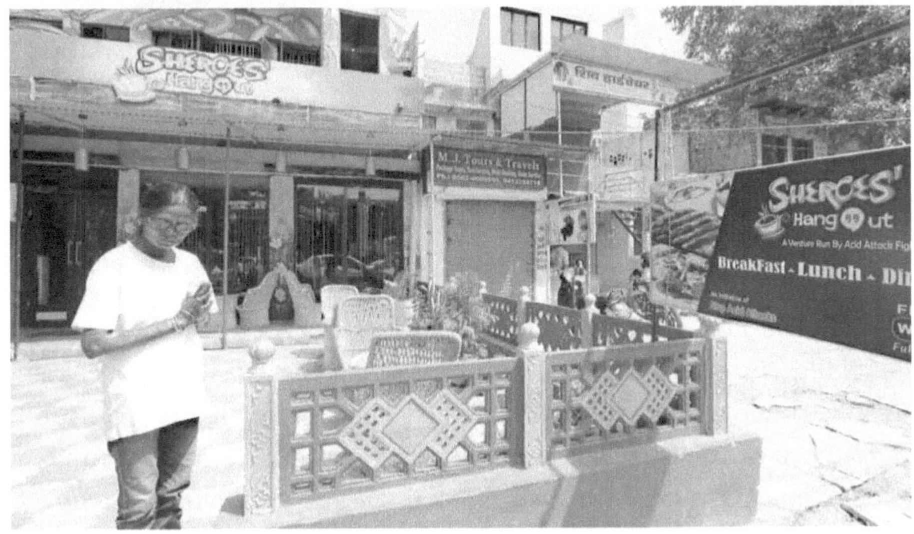

Pic 3:

Inside of the Hangout: Readers' Café, Library and Exhibition-cum-sale point (file photo)

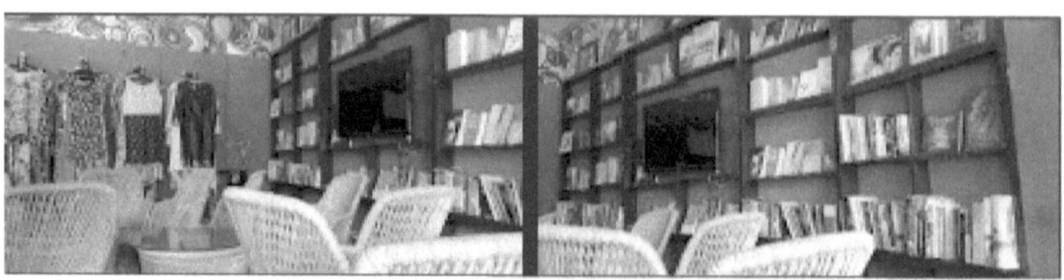

Pic 4:

Ritu, Rupa and Neetu...the stars with scars!! (file photo)

What Corporates can do? As a first step towards a good gesture, corporate companies may contemplate inviting the Sheroes to their offices and organize interactions with them, which would provide an opportunity to all those on their rolls, more so to their invaluable woman force, to listen to and learn from the inspirational tales of the Sheroes...on how to combat such a situation in real life. Needless to say, the interaction with the Sheroes will present them with the opportunity to directly listen from the horses' mouths and learn from their real-life stories, which will be distinctly different from the celluloid's bland and insipid reel-life stories. The sharing of their experience by the Sheroes themselves from the stage can provide a real thrust that can tremendously impact the corporate minds against the atrocities on women making them resolute in their endeavor to wipe out this terrible malady from the face of the country, and ultimately, from every nook and corner of the planet as a whole.

A New Definition to the feminine world: The Sheroes have given a new definition to the feminine world. Through their matchless actions, they have shown that the women of India will not succumb to any brutality... however severe it might be. Through their exemplary courage of par excellence, they have demonstrated what the woman power in the country can do and become. Through their steely resolve, they have shown how not to yield to circumstances but fight back. Despite the severity of the crime they were subjected to by society, still they preferred to extend their compassion to society and did not nurture any ill feelings against those who caused them unfathomable pain and suffering. This particular quality of theirs was evident as we found them in all smiles, during our interaction. We noticed not even a shade of gloom on their faces. Their faces were sparkling with radiance! They truly represent the valiant woman of this great country. Their everlasting action has placed the entire womanhood at the zenith in the social order. Let's salute these women with exceptional individuality, a trait which needs to be acquired by every woman irrespective of the place/region she belongs to.

How to reach Sheroes? Sheroes' Hangout is presently located behind the Go Stops Hostel, Taj Nagari Phase 1, R.K. Puram Phase-2, Tajganj, Agra, Uttar Pradesh 282001. *Contact Number:*99580 66951 (the mobile number belongs to Ajeet, who provided me the details of the new address when I spoke to him recently). The Sheroes can be reached by e-mail at *sheroes.hangout@gmail.com*. On inquiry, it is gathered that now the hangout has started another unit in Lucknow which is being run by another 10 acid attack survivors (both male and female). The Hangout is also on Facebook (from where I have downloaded the file photos and compiled more details about the Sheroes).

In Oct 2015, when we visited the Sheroes, the Hangout was located opposite The Gateway Hotel, Taj View Chowraha, Fatehabad Road, Tajganj, Agra, Uttar Pradesh 282001. Phone: 0562-4000 401, 75330 83502.

Why I am sharing this story? With due thanks to the TV-9 Telugu channel for airing the extraordinary story about the Sheroes way back on one night during the winter of Sept 2015, the idea behind sharing this precious and priceless story is to garner support for the Sheroes, and several such other women, who are showing the way to live. Needless to say, the Sheroes are the epitomes of success and living examples of supreme bravery, and signify victory over evil, providing beacons of light to the countless hapless victims of the mindless acid attacks, happening at regular intervals around us.

What you can do in return, to help them continue their stupendous cause? You may contemplate doing something similar as a fitting tribute to the brave sheroes, the living inspiration to countless hapless women, who are silently suffering the untold atrocities caused on them day in and day out. You can provide the sheroes *found in the vicinity of where you are* with the required might to help them combat life's worst battles they are into, thereby empowering them to come out of their grief and lead a life with dignity.

It's time to take this important decision NOW, and simultaneously act upon it by putting your heart and soul into it! Are You Ready To Do So?

--//--

References

1. Human Values in Management – By Swami Ranganathananda

2. The Impact of Science on Society – By Bertrand Russell

3. A Manifesto for Change-A sequel to India 2020 – By Dr. APJ Abdul Kalam

4. You are born to Blossom – By Dr. APJ Abdul Kalam

5. The Guiding Light – By Dr. APJ Abdul Kalam

6. The Ignited Minds-Unleashing the power within India – By Dr APJ Abdul Kalam

7. India-2020 – By Dr. APJ Abdul Kalam

8. Meditations – By Marcus Aurelius

9. The Mahabharata – By C. Rajagopalachari

10. The Ramayana – By C. Rajagopalachari

11. The Panchatantra – By Vishnusarma and translated from Sanskrit by Chandra Rajan, Penguin Classics

12. Thirukkural – By Thiruvalluvar, with transliteration by Rev W.H. Drew, Rev John Lazarus

13. Kautilya's Arthashastra, the 2021 publication by Fingerprint Classics/New Delhi

14. Lao Tzu's Tao Te Ching – By Ursula K. Le Guin, published by Colossal Publications

15. Website of Hislop College and other related research material

16. Different social media platforms

17. The NIV Bible (Source:https://www.beautifulchristianlife.com/blog/why-wisdom-is-far-more-valuable-than-intelligence)

Eternal Quotes Of:

Abraham Lincoln	Charles Dickens	Nelson Mandela
Albert Einstein	Erol Ozan	Natheniel Adebesin
Dr. APJ Abdul Kalam	Epicurus	Ratan Tata
Alfred Lord Tennyson	Edmond Burke	Ralph Waldo Emerson
A.R. Rahman	Herman Hesse	Swami Ranganathananda
Aldous Huxley	John F Kennedy	Sri Sathya Sai Baba
Anthony Douglas Williams	J Robert Oppenheimer	Stephen William Hawking
Sri Adi Shankara	Jimi Hendrix	Dr T.P. Chia
St. Augustine	Mahatma Gandhi	T.S. Eliot
Sri Aurabindo	Mother Theresa	Swami Vivekananda
Bertrand Russell	Martin Luther King Jr	William Wordsworth
Confucius	Marcus Aurelius	Zat Rana

--//--